SAMUEL TAYLOR COLERIDGE.
After a portrait painted in 1795.

The Academy Classics

# THREE NARRATIVE POEMS

COLERIDGE: THE RIME OF THE ANCIENT MARINER
ARNOLD: SOHRAB AND RUSTUM
TENNYSON: ENOCH ARDEN

EDITED BY

GEORGE A. WATROUS, A.M.

ALLYN AND BACON
Boston      New York      Chicago

Norwood Press
J. S. Cushing & Co. — Berwick & Smith
Norwood Mass. U.S.A.

# PREFACE.

The purpose of this volume of the *Academy Series* is to offer in a single book the three narrative poems set by the New York Regents for a part of second-year English. It is believed that the nature of the poems readily admits such grouping, and that the combination will be a convenience for teachers and a saving for students. Schools which offer only the reading required for entrance to college, and would therefore need only *The Ancient Mariner*, may find the present volume of advantage, in that its use will permit the student to make comparison with other narrative compositions. The text has been carefully chosen in each instance.

The editor gratefully acknowledges his obligations to other workers in the same field. The plan of the book is his own, but in the execution of that plan many sources have been freely drawn upon. The aim in the preparation of the notes has been to suggest to the student such other reading as will help him to interpret for himself the poem in hand. The map to make clear the geography of *Sohrab and Rustum* was made by Miss Alice Derfla Howes, to whom the editor would also acknowledge his gratitude for valuable suggestions embodied in the notes.

G. A. W.

Utica Free Academy,
    October, 1898.

iii

16332

# CONTENTS.

# SAMUEL TAYLOR COLERIDGE.

## (1772–1834.)

THE life of Coleridge, though abounding in interesting detail, may be briefly summarized. He was a precocious child. His father was an eccentric man, a country curate, always tormented by poverty, yet always earnest and true! He it was who sought to simplify Latin grammar, and among other changes intended to smooth the beginner's way, proposed to call the ablative the quare-quale-quiddi-tive case. His successor in the parish was reproached because in his sermons he did not quote the immediate language of the Holy Spirit, by which name the Reverend Coleridge had described the Hebrew wherewith he had delighted his innocent parishioners.

When Samuel was nine years old his father died, and the boy was placed in Christ's Hospital. Here began a friendship that endured throughout life — that with Charles Lamb. Here, too, was first apparent Coleridge's wonderful fascination in conversation. He was wretched there, as all boys were. How unhappy we may know from Lamb's famous essay, *Christ's Hospital Five and Thirty Years' Ago*. At regular intervals the gates of the school were closed against all the lads for a day. This time they might spend with friends in the city. Coleridge had none; but he was excluded with the others, and passed the day wandering aimlessly about the great, lonely city. He was fond of swimming, and in summer time enjoyed this exercise on these days of banishment. On one occasion he fell into the water with his clothes on, and returning to the school at the appointed hour was soundly flogged and compelled to wear his wet apparel until it dried. One of his biographers suggests that here was laid the foundation of the physical ailment that later drove him to the opium habit. If this be true, surely he was as much sinned against as sinning.

Coleridge spent eight or nine years at Christ's Hospital, and then entered Jesus College, Cambridge (1791). His university career is almost a blank. In 1792 he gained the gold medal for a Greek ode. This argues that in the first years of his course he applied himself to his work. Soon, however, is evident the lack of concentration that later in life characterized all he undertook. Poetry, medicine, and metaphysics successively engaged his mind to the exclusion of all else. He became discontented, and finally left the university secretly and went to London. The night of his arrival he passed in the streets, and the next morning enlisted in a regiment of dragoons under the name Silas Titus Cumberback. His classical learning betrayed him, however, and his friends secured his release. But his university career was ended. Shortly after he was married to Sara Fricker, sister of Southey's wife. For a time his domestic relations were happy, but later, when the opium habit had fastened itself upon him, he left his family and never lived with them again. A pension given by the Wedgewoods enabled him to study in Germany. Something more than a year he spent in mastering the language and in studying metaphysics. When he returned he brought the manuscript of his translation of Schiller's *Wallenstein*, which had been recently published. In 1804 he went to Malta as secretary to the governor. He visited

Rome, and in August, 1806, returned to England. During his absence Coleridge was a bad correspondent. But once or twice did his family hear from him directly. When he returned his indifference gradually became more marked. After a short visit with his wife and children, when there seems to have been a slight effort to restore friendly relations, he took refuge with Wordsworth at Coleorton.

The opium habit was now fixed upon him, and the next few years record his resolute struggles against the vice and his craven yielding to its power. In October, 1810, he went to London, and there, penniless, miserable, alone, he continued the battle. He lectured on Shakespeare and Milton, brought out his *Remorse*, wrote for newspapers, and prepared *Biographia Literaria*. In it all he was irregular and fitful — opium had too strong a hold on him. At last in despair he voluntarily placed himself under the care of Dr Gillman at Highgate. This was in 1816, and here he passed the rest of his life, free from the curse of his bondage. He worked constantly, and, under the loving care of the Gillmans, grew stronger in body and more spiritual in mind. *Christabel, Remorse, Zapolya, Sibylline Leaves, The Three Graves*, and *Aids to Reflection* were published during these last years. The house of the Gillmans became a place of resort for the literary circle in London. The charm of his conversation delighted his hearers; their presence comforted the poet. On the 25th of July, 1834, he died. His grave is at Highgate, and above it is the epitaph written by himself in 1833.

In his lifetime Coleridge was not appreciated. From *Lyrical Ballads* to *Sibylline Leaves* adverse criticism greeted his efforts. It was reserved for a later generation to recognize his wonderful genius. The shadow of his weakness obscured the splendor of his greatness. To us his versatility and inimitable mastery of language strongly appeal. His style always accords with his subject. The energetic wildness of the *Ancient Mariner, Christabel's* supernatural witchery, and the unrivalled grandeur of the *Hymn to Mont Blanc* are distinct in theme and style. Each has a liquid melody of diction unsurpassed in literature, and there is a nervous strength of expression that makes every sentence a picture. In his originality we may see one reason why he was not sooner appreciated. "Originality is like a new coin; people hardly know its real worth, and they hesitate to receive it." The work of many poets bears out the truth of this assertion.

The distinctive characteristic of all that Coleridge wrote is the spirit of love that pervades his work. The words of the *Ancient Mariner* express the feeling he ever delighted to cherish. Universal benevolence possessed his heart, and all creation, to him, teemed with life and beauty.

# MATTHEW ARNOLD.

### (1822–1888.)

MATTHEW ARNOLD was born at Laleham, Middlesex County, England, December 24, 1822. He was educated under the most favorable circumstances, entering Rugby in 1837, where his father was so long head master. A few years later he went to Balliol College, Oxford. Here he was associated with the Froudes, Principal Shairp, Chief Justice Coleridge, Bishop Fraser, Dean Church, John Henry Newman, Arthur Hugh Clough, and Thomas Hughes. Even among such men his ability as a student made him at once conspicuous. In 1840 he won a Latin scholarship; in 1843, with a poem on Cromwell, he captured the Newdigate prize;

and, in 1844, he was made Fellow of Oriel, just thirty years after the same honor had been conferred on his father. In 1851 he was appointed one of the Inspectors of Schools — a position in which he exerted a far-reaching influence for the improvement of England's educational system.

Arnold's first literary venture was with a volume of poetry, *The Strayed Reveller and Other Poems*, published in 1848, and signed "A." By this and his two succeeding volumes, *Empedocles on Etna and Other Poems*, 1852, and *Poems: a New Edition*, 1853, he secured recognition as a poet. It was more than ten years after these efforts before he appeared as a critic of literature. In this field he gained his greatest renown; he is greater as a critic than as a poet. In 1857 he was elected Professor of Poetry at Oxford, and four years later published his lectures *On Translating Homer*. From this time on he wrote constantly on a wide range of subjects. All, however, tended toward a single aim — "the arousing of a better intellectual feeling in the life of England, literary, religious, political." He lectured frequently, and twice visited the United States. He criticised severely our "money-getting" mania, but not more severely than he condemned England's weaknesses. His greatest work, *Essays in Criticism*, appeared in 1865. It was followed by volumes on religious questions. *St. Paul and Protestantism*, *Literature and Dogma*, *God and the Bible*, and *Last Essays on Church and State* give us the result of his mature consideration of these themes. He twice received the degree LL.D.: from Edinburgh, 1869, and Oxford, 1870. He died in 1888, very suddenly and peacefully, of heart disease.

We may not agree with his conclusions in criticism or in religious speculation, but we recognize in him a man of the highest culture, a scholar of extraordinary attainments, an educational reformer, an acute critic, and, above all, a good man.

As a critic he devoted himself to authors and their books in a general way. Rarely did he criticise any book in particular. He considered the impression made as a whole, estimated books and men in the totality, and infused into this criticism his own attractive personality. It was he who introduced the *causerie* or chat, and with it that constant reiteration which often irritates, yet never fails of effecting its aim.

In poetry as in criticism, he exalted the ideal element in human character. Its presence and power were to him the essentials of true living. He defined his idea of poetry, and as an index of the spirit that ruled the author of *Sohrab and Rustum*, we can do no better than to repeat his words. "The radical difference," he says, "between the poetic theory of the Greeks and our own is this: that with them the poetical character of the action in itself, and the conduct of it, was the first consideration; with us, attention is fixed mainly on the value of the separate thoughts and images which occur in the treatment of an action. They regarded the whole; we regard the parts. We have poems which seem to exist merely for the sake of single lines and passages, and not for the sake of producing any total impression."

Here, then, is the key to his method. No better exposition of his doctrine could be offered than a reading of *Balder Dead*, *Tristam and Iseult*, and *Sohrab and Rustum*. It must not be thought that Arnold despised details of diction, rhythm, and other technical elements that beautify verse. On the contrary he was exceedingly careful of these effects. His smoothly flowing pentameters, brilliant aphorisms, and stately figures are evidence sufficient. But he never confused the means with the end. The total effect of an entire composition was to him an ever-present consideration, and the chief aim of his endeavor. This is evident in his shorter poems no less than in the longer narrative pieces. His sonnets, lyric and dramatic poems, and his elegiac verses show clearly that he felt at the beginning what he wished the reader to feel when he had done. Indeed, if so technical a term may be pardoned, it has always seemed to the present writer that the first verse of any poem by Arnold might be fitly named a topic sentence for a paragraph that embraced the whole poem. It is in this that his chief charm consists. From this came the ease of composition, the purity of diction, and the simple strength of figure that distinguish his verse. He was a classical man, thoroughly imbued with the spirit of Greek culture, and to the modern world he has given some of its purest poetic ideals and realities.

## ALFRED, LORD TENNYSON.

### (1809–1892.)

TENNYSON was born August 6, 1809, at Somersby, a small parish of Lincolnshire, of which his father was the rector. He was one of twelve children, the third of eight brothers in a family characterized by poetic genius. In 1828 Alfred and his brother Charles entered Trinity College, Cambridge, but left, after the death of their father (1831), without taking degrees. At Cambridge began the friendship with Arthur Hallam, whose early death had a profound influence over Tennyson's life and work. In 1850, his "annus mirabilis," Tennyson was married to Emily Sellwood, published *In Memoriam*, and was appointed poet-laureate. He settled at Twickenham, three years later removed to Farringford, near Freshwater, and still later (1867) he bought the estate of Aldworth in Sussex. Here he resided until his death, October 6, 1892.

Tennyson's first volume was published in 1830. The title was *Poems, Chiefly Lyrical.* Two years later came his second collection, and in these poems we can now recognize the germs of the perfect workmanship and exquisite melody which characterized his mature work. He was criticised severely. Reviews of that day called him effeminate and sentimental, but the popular voice gave him an enthusiastic welcome, and he was at once received as a poet.

Several causes operated in effecting this immediate recognition. He had no serious rivals. Wordsworth, Southey, and Coleridge had passed the prime of their poetic powers; Keats, Shelley, and Byron, who had been much nearer the the hearts of the people, were dead, and "the fruit of public acceptance was once more ripe for plucking." Greater, however, than this negative influence was the positive power of Tennyson's versatility. Gradually his perfection in art disarmed his critics. He became the man of the hour, and presented in his poems the thought and feeling of the day. The themes were simple, the poems short and easily understood.

In 1859 four poems, entitled *Idylls of the King,* were published. Each poem was independent of its companion poems, yet each presented the same group of characters, the knights and ladies of King Arthur's court. From time to time during the next twenty-five years Tennyson added to this group, and the completed poem, consisting of twelve parts, constitutes his greatest work. It may be properly called an epic, though it is sometimes described as a collection of idylls. King Arthur is taken as the type of true manhood in its struggle against the evil of the world, and thus the poem takes something of the nature of an allegory. *The Coming of Arthur* tells us how the prince secured his throne. Then follow ten poems relating the deeds of his knights; and last, *The Passing of Arthur* records the great battle in which the hero was so sorely wounded that he was borne away from earth to be healed.

The limits of the present sketch forbid more than a mention of a few of the laureate's other poems. *The Princess,* in which Tennyson is supposed to have set forth his views on the higher education of woman, appeared in 1842. With *Maud,* a somewhat sentimental romance in verse, *The Charge of the Light Brigade* and an *Ode on the Death of the Duke of Wellington* were published (1855). *Enoch Arden and Other Poems* (1864) contained, beside the longer poem, the *Northern Farmer, Aylmer's Field, Tithonus, Sea Dreams,* and *Lucretius. De Profundis, The Defence of Lucknow, The Revenge, Tiresias,* and many of his minor pieces, belong to the poet's later life.

Tennyson often doubted that his poetic achievements would endure. Looking at Aldworth one time with Mr. Knowles, its architect, he said: "That house will last longer than I shall. It will last five hundred years." This uncertainty led the poet to attempt dramatic composition, a work for which his genius was ill adapted. Occasional passages and scenes are dramatic, yet the plays are essentially poems upon which the dramatic form has been forced. Henry Irving and Miss Bateman in *Queen Mary* and the Kendals in *The Falcon* could not save these dramas from dismal failure. *Harold, Becket, The Promise of May,* and *The Cup,* though admirably staged and presented with strong casts, shared the same fate. *The Foresters,* a romantic, pastoral play, published in 1892, achieved considerable success when presented by Mr. Daly in New York, with Ada Rehan as Maid Marian. The laureate's fame gained no fresh laurels through his ventures in the field of the drama.

Such is the outline of a life and work wonderfully complete. Tennyson was a born poet. "He lisped in numbers," published verses while a mere lad, wrote a prize poem at Cambridge, and published when he was more than eighty years old. Throughout his life he stood high in popular esteem and favor. He secured what most men fail to receive — a reward of praise while living. He was a learned man, happy in his family, and honored by the world. Oxford gave him her highest mark of esteem, the honorary degree of D.C.L. He refused a baronetcy, but later became a lord. In narrative, lyric, and monodramatic verse he is unrivalled; in the *Idylls of the King* he gave us an epic on a subject of national interest, but his attempts at dramatic composition were less successful. His life was fully rounded — full of labor and replete with honors.

SAMUEL TAYLOR COLERIDGE

# THE RIME OF THE ANCIENT MARINER

# THE RIME OF THE ANCIENT MARINER.

## PART I.

It is an ancient Mariner,
And he stoppeth one of three.
"By thy long gray beard and glittering eye,
Now wherefore stopp'st thou me?

"The Bridegroom's doors are opened wide,    **5**
And I am next of kin;
The guests are met, the feast is set:
Mayst hear the merry din."

He holds him with his skinny hand,
"There was a ship," quoth he.    **10**
"Hold off! unhand me, graybeard loon!"
Eftsoons his hand dropt he.

He holds him with his glittering eye —
The Wedding Guest stood still,
And listens like a three-years' child:    **15**
The Mariner hath his will.

The Wedding Guest sat on a stone;
He cannot choose but hear;
And thus spake on that ancient man,
The bright-eyed Mariner:—    **20**

"The ship was cheered, the harbor cleared,
Merrily did we drop
Below the kirk, below the hill,
Below the lighthouse top.

"The sun came up upon the left,                    25
Out of the sea came he!
And he shone bright, and on the right
Went down into the sea.

"Higher and higher every day,
Till over the mast at noon"—                       30
The Wedding Guest here beat his breast,
For he heard the loud bassoon.

The bride hath paced into the hall,
Red as a rose is she;
Nodding their heads before her, goes              35
The merry minstrelsy.

The Wedding Guest he beat his breast,
Yet he cannot choose but hear;
And thus spake on that ancient man,
The bright-eyed Mariner:—                          40

"And now the storm blast came, and he
Was tyrannous and strong:
He struck with his o'ertaking wings,
And chased us south along.

"With sloping masts and dipping prow,             45
As who pursued with yell and blow
Still treads the shadow of his foe,

And forward bends his head,
The ship drove fast, loud roared the blast,
And southward aye we fled.        50

" And now there came both mist and snow,
And it grew wondrous cold,
And ice, mast-high, came floating by,
As green as emerald.

" And through the drifts the snowy clifts        55
Did send a dismal sheen :
Nor shapes of men nor beasts we ken —
The ice was all between.

" The ice was here, the ice was there,
The ice was all around :        60
It cracked and growled, and roared and howled,
Like noises in a swound !

" At length did cross an Albatross :
Thorough the fog it came ;
As if it had been a Christian soul,        65
We hailed it in God's name.

" It ate the food it ne'er had eat,
And round and round it flew.
The ice did split with a thunder fit ;
The helmsmen steered us through !        70

" And a good south wind sprung up behind ;
The Albatross did follow,
And every day, for food or play,
Came to the mariners' hollo !

"In mist or cloud, on mast or shroud,          75
It perched for vespers nine;
Whiles all the night, through fog smoke white,
Glimmered the white moonshine."

"God save thee, ancient Mariner,
From the fiends that plague thee thus!          80
Why look'st thou so?"—"With my crossbow
I shot the Albatross."

## PART II.

"The Sun now rose upon the right,
Out of the sea came he,
Still hid in mist, and on the left          85
Went down into the sea.

"And the good south wind still blew behind,
But no sweet bird did follow,
Nor any day, for food or play,
Came to the mariners' hollo!          90

"And I had done a hellish thing,
And it would work 'em woe:
For all averred, I had killed the bird
That made the breeze to blow.
'Ah, wretch!' said they, 'the bird to slay,          95
That made the breeze to blow!'

"Nor dim nor red, like God's own head,
The glorious Sun uprist;
Then all averred, I had killed the bird

That brought the fog and mist.        100
' 'Twas right,' said they, ' such birds to slay,
That bring the fog and mist.'

" The fair breeze blew, the white foam flew,
The furrow followed free ;
We were the first that ever burst        105
Into that silent sea.

" Down dropt the breeze, the sails dropt down,
'Twas sad as sad could be ;
And we did speak only to break
The silence of the sea !        110

" All in a hot and copper sky,
The bloody Sun, at noon,
Right up above the mast did stand,
No bigger than the Moon.

" Day after day, day after day,        115
We stuck, nor breath nor motion;
As idle as a painted ship
Upon a painted ocean.

" Water, water, everywhere,
And all the boards did shrink;        120
Water, water, everywhere,
Nor any drop to drink.

" The very deep did rot, O Christ !
That ever this should be !
Yea, slimy things did crawl with legs        125
Upon the slimy sea.

" About, about, in reel and rout,
The death-fires danced at night;
The water, like a witch's oils,
Burnt green, and blue, and white.          130

" And some in dreams assurèd were
Of the spirit that plagued us so;
Nine fathom deep he had followed us
From the land of mist and snow.

" And every tongue, through utter drought,    135
Was withered at the root;
We could not speak, no more than if
We had been choked with soot.

" Ah, welladay ! what evil looks
Had I from old and young !            140
Instead of the cross, the Albatross
About my neck was hung."


## PART III.

" There passed a weary time.   Each throat
Was parched, and glazed each eye.
A weary time ! a weary time !         145
How glazed each weary eye !
When looking westward I beheld
A something in the sky.

" At first it seemed a little speck,
And then it seemed a mist.           150
It moved and moved, and took at last
A certain shape, I wist.

"A speck, a mist, a shape, I wist!
And still it neared and neared:
As if it dodged a water sprite,          155
It plunged and tacked and veered.

"With throats unslaked, with black lips baked,
We could nor laugh nor wail;
Through utter drought all dumb we stood!
I bit my arm, I sucked the blood,          160
And cried, 'A sail! a sail!'

"With throats unslaked, with black lips baked,
Agape they heard me call.
Gramercy! they for joy did grin,
And all at once their breath drew in,          165
As they were drinking all.

"'See! see!' I cried, 'she tacks no more
Hither, to work us weal —
Without a breeze, without a tide,
She steadies with upright keel!'          170

"The western wave was all aflame,
The day was well-nigh done,
Almost upon the western wave
Rested the broad bright Sun;
When that strange shape drove suddenly          175
Betwixt us and the Sun.

"And straight the Sun was flecked with bars,
(Heaven's Mother send us grace!)
As if through a dungeon grate he peered,
With broad and burning face.          180

"'Alas!' thought I, and my heart beat loud,
'How fast she nears and nears!
Are those her sails that glance in the Sun,
Like restless gossameres?

"'Are those her ribs through which the Sun　185
Did peer, as through a grate?
And is that Woman all her crew?
Is that a Death? and are there two?
Is Death that Woman's mate?'

"Her lips were red, her looks were free,　190
Her locks were yellow as gold:
Her skin was as white as leprosy,
The Nightmare Life-in-Death was she,
Who thicks man's blood with cold.

"The naked hulk alongside came,　195
And the twain were casting dice:
'The game is done! I've won, I've won!'
Quoth she, and whistles thrice.

"The Sun's rim dips; the stars rush out:
At one stride comes the dark;　200
With far-heard whisper, o'er the sea,
Off shot the specter bark.

"We listened, and looked sideways up!
Fear at my heart, as at a cup,
My lifeblood seemed to sip!　205
The stars were dim, and thick the night;
The steersman's face by his lamp gleamed white;

From the sails the dew did drip,
Till clomb above the eastern bar
The hornèd Moon, with one bright **star**    210
Within the nether tip.

"One after one, by the star-dogged **Moon,**
Too quick for groan or sigh,
Each turned his face with a ghastly **pang,**
And cursed me with his eye.    215

"Four times fifty living men
(And I heard nor sigh nor groan),
With heavy thump, a lifeless lump,
They dropped down one by one.

"The souls did from their bodies **fly,**—    220
They fled to bliss or woe!
And every soul, it passed me by
Like the whiz of my crossbow!"

## PART IV.

'I fear thee, ancient Mariner!
I fear thy skinny hand!    225
And thou art long and lank and **brown,**
As is the ribbed sea sand.

"I fear thee and thy glittering eye,
And thy skinny hand, so brown!"—
"Fear not, fear not, thou Wedding **Guest!**    230
This body dropped not down.

"Alone, alone, all, all alone,
Alone on a wide, wide sea!
And never a saint took pity on
My soul in agony.                                          235

"The many men, so beautiful!
And they all dead did lie!
And a thousand thousand slimy things
Lived on; and so did I.

"I looked upon the rotting sea,                            240
And drew my eyes away:
I looked upon the rotting deck,
And there the dead men lay.

"I looked to heaven, and tried to pray;
But or ever a prayer had gusht,                            245
A wicked whisper came, and made
My heart as dry as dust.

"I closed my lids, and kept them close,
And the balls like pulses beat;
For the sky and the sea, and the sea and the sky, 250
Lay like a load on my weary eye,
And the dead were at my feet.

"The cold sweat melted from their limbs,
Nor rot nor reek did they:
The look with which they looked on me                      255
Had never passed away.

"An orphan's curse would drag to hell
A spirit from on high;
But oh! more horrible than that

Is the curse in a dead man's eye!                    260
Seven days, seven nights, I saw that curse,
And yet I could not die.

"The moving Moon went up the sky,
And nowhere did abide:
Softly she was going up,                             265
And a star or two beside.

"Her beams bemocked the sultry main,
Like April hoarfrost spread;
But where the ship's huge shadow lay,
The charmèd water burnt alway                        270
A still and awful red.

"Beyond the shadow of the ship
I watched the water snakes:
They moved in tracks of shining white,
And when they reared, the elfish light               275
Fell off in hoary flakes.

"Within the shadow of the ship
I watched their rich attire:
Blue, glossy green, and velvet black,
They coiled and swam; and every track                280
Was a flash of golden fire.

" O happy living things! no tongue
Their beauty might declare:
A spring of love gushed from my heart,
And I blessed them unaware!                           285
Sure my kind saint took pity on me,
And I blessed them unaware.

" The selfsame moment I could pray;
And from my neck so free
The Albatross fell off, and sank                    290
Like lead into the sea."


## PART V.

"O sleep! it is a gentle thing,
Beloved from pole to pole!
To Mary Queen the praise be given!
She sent the gentle sleep from heaven,               295
That slid into my soul.

" The silly buckets on the deck,
That had so long remained,
I dreamt that they were filled with dew;
And when I awoke, it rained.                          300

" My lips were wet, my throat was cold,
My garments all were dank;
Sure I had drunken in my dreams,
And still my body drank.

" I moved, and could not feel my limbs               305
I was so light — almost
I thought that I had died in sleep,
And was a blessèd ghost.

" And soon I heard a roaring wind:
It did not come anear;                               310
But with its sound it shook the sails,
That were so thin and sere.

" The upper air burst into life !
And a hundred fire flags sheen,
To and fro they were hurried about;          315
And to and fro, and in and out,
The wan stars danced between.

" And the coming wind did roar more loud,
And the sails did sigh like sedge;
And the rain poured down from one black cloud; 320
The Moon was at its edge.

" The thick black cloud was cleft, and still
The Moon was at its side:
Like waters shot from some high crag,
The lightning fell with never a jag,          325
A river steep and wide.

" The loud wind never reached the ship,
Yet now the ship moved on !
Beneath the lightning and the Moon
The dead men gave a groan.                    330

" They groaned, they stirred, they all uprose,
Nor spake, nor moved their eyes ;
It had been strange, even in a dream,
To have seen those dead men rise.

" The helmsman steered, the ship moved on ;   335
Yet never a breeze upblew ;
The mariners all 'gan work the ropes,
Where they were wont to do ;
They raised their limbs like lifeless tools —
We were a ghastly crew.                       340

"The body of my brother's son
Stood by me, knee to knee!
The body and I pulled at one rope,
But he said naught to me."

"I fear thee, ancient Mariner!" —  345
"Be calm, thou Wedding Guest!
'Twas not those souls that fled in pain
Which to their corses came again,
But a troop of spirits blest.

"For when it dawned, they dropped their arms,  350
And clustered round the mast;
Sweet sounds rose slowly through their mouths,
And from their bodies passed.

"Around, around, flew each sweet sound,
Then darted to the Sun;  355
Slowly the sounds came back again,
Now mixed, now one by one.

"Sometimes adropping from the sky
I heard the skylark sing;
Sometimes all little birds that are,  360
How they seemed to fill the sea and air
With their sweet jargoning!

"And now 'twas like all instruments,
Now like a lonely flute;
And now it is an angel's song,  365
That makes the heavens be mute.

"It ceased; yet still the sails made on
A pleasant noise till noon,
A noise like of a hidden brook
In the leafy month of June,                        370
That to the sleeping woods all night
Singeth a quiet tune.

"Till noon we quietly sailed on,
Yet never a breeze did breathe:
Slowly and smoothly went the ship,                 375
Moved onward from beneath.

"Under the keel nine fathom deep,
From the land of mist and snow,
The spirit slid: and it was he
That made the ship to go.                           380
The sails at noon left off their tune,
And the ship stood still also.

"The Sun, right up above the mast,
Had fixed her to the ocean:
But in a minute she 'gan stir                       385
With a short uneasy motion—
Backwards and forwards half her length,
With a short uneasy motion.

"Then, like a pawing horse let go,
She made a sudden bound:                            390
It flung the blood into my head,        ✗ action
And I fell down in a swound.

"How long in that same fit I lay,
I have not to declare;

c

But ere my living life returned,                          395
I heard, and in my soul discerned,
Two voices in the air.

"'Is it he?' quoth one, 'is this the man?
By Him who died on cross,
With his cruel bow he laid full low          400
The harmless Albatross.

"'The spirit who bideth by himself
In the land of mist and snow,
He loved the bird that loved the man
Who shot him with his bow.'                    405

"The other was a softer voice.
As soft as honeydew:
Quoth he, 'The man hath penance done,
And penance more will do.'"


## PART VI.

### First Voice.

"'But tell me, tell me! speak again,           41C
Thy soft response renewing, —
What makes that ship drive on so fast?
What is the Ocean doing?'

### Second Voice.

"'Still as a slave before his lord,
The Ocean hath no blast;                         415
His great bright eye most silently
Up to the Moon is cast,

" ' If he may know which way to go;
For she guides him, smooth or grim.
See, brother, see ! how graciously          420
She looketh down on him.'

### First Voice.

" ' But why drives on that ship so fast,
Without or wave or wind ? '

### Second Voice.

" ' The air is cut away before,
And closes from behind.          425

" ' Fly, brother, fly ! more high, more high !
Or we shall be belated;
For slow and slow that ship will go,
When the Mariner's trance is abated.'

" I woke, and we were sailing on,          430
As in a gentle weather:
'Twas night, calm night, the Moon was high;
The dead men stood together.

" All stood together on the deck,
For a charnel dungeon fitter:          435
All fixed on me their stony eyes,
That in the Moon did glitter.

" The pang, the curse, with which they died,
Had never passed away :
I could not draw my eyes from theirs,          440
Nor turn them up to pray.

"And now this spell was snapt: once more
I viewed the ocean green,
And looked far forth, yet little saw
Of what had else been seen —                    445


"Like one that on a lonesome road
Doth walk in fear and dread,
And having once turned round walks on,
And turns no more his head,
Because he knows a frightful fiend            450
Doth close behind him tread.


"But soon there breathed a wind on me,
Nor sound nor motion made:
Its path was not upon the sea,
In ripple or in shade.                         455


"It raised my hair, it fanned my cheek
Like a meadow-gale of spring —
It mingled strangely with my fears,
Yet it felt like a welcoming.


"Swiftly, swiftly, flew the ship,             460
Yet she sailed softly too;
Sweetly, sweetly, blew the breeze —
On me alone it blew.


"Oh, dream of joy! is this indeed
The lighthouse top I see?                      465
Is this the hill? is this the kirk?
Is this mine own countree?

" We drifted o'er the harbor bar,
And I with sobs did pray, —
'O let me be awake, my God!     470
Or let me sleep alway.'

" The harbor bay was clear as glass,
So smoothly it was strewn;
And on the bay the moonlight lay,
And the shadow of the Moon.     475

" The rock shone bright, the kirk no less,
That stands above the rock:
The moonlight steeped in silentness
The steady weathercock.

" And the bay was white with silent light,     480
Till, rising from the same,
Full many shapes, that shadows were,
In crimson colors came.

" A little distance from the prow
Those crimson shadows were:     485
I turned my eyes upon the deck —
O Christ! what saw I there!

" Each corse lay flat, lifeless and **flat,**
And, by the holy rood!
A man all light, a seraph man,     490
On every corse there stood.

" This seraph band, each waved his hand:
It was a heavenly sight!
They stood as signals to the land,
Each one a lovely light;     495

"This seraph band, each waved his hand.
No voice did they impart, —
No voice; but oh! the silence sank
Like music on my heart.

"But soon I heard the dash of oars,　　　　　50(
I heard the Pilot's cheer;
My head was turned perforce away,
And I saw a boat appear.

"The Pilot, and the Pilot's boy,
I heard them coming fast —　　　　　505
Dear Lord in heaven! it was a joy
The dead men could not blast.

"I saw a third — I heard his voice:
It is the Hermit good!
He singeth loud his godly hymns　　　　　510
That he makes in the wood.
He'll shrieve my soul, he'll wash away
The Albatross's blood."

# PART VII.

"This Hermit good lives in that wood
Which slopes down to the sea.　　　　　515
How loudly his sweet voice he rears!
He loves to talk with marineres
That come from a far countree.

"He kneels at morn and noon and eve:
He hath a cushion plump:　　　　　520
It is the moss that wholly hides
The rotted old oak stump.

"The skiff boat neared; I heard them talk
'Why, this is strange, I trow!
Where are those lights so many and fair,      525
That signal made but now?'

"'Strange, by my faith!' the Hermit said:
'And they answered not our cheer!
The planks look warped! and see those sails,
How thin they are and sere!                   530
I never saw aught like to them,
Unless perchance it were

"'Brown skeletons of leaves that lag
My forest brook along;
When the ivy tod is heavy with snow,          535
And the owlet whoops to the wolf below,
That eats the she-wolf's young.'

"'Dear Lord! it hath a fiendish look,'
The Pilot made reply:
'I am afeared.'—'Push on, push on!'          540
Said the Hermit cheerily.

"The boat came closer to the ship,
But I nor spake nor stirred;
The boat came close beneath the ship,
And straight a sound was heard.               545

"Under the water it rumbled on,
Still louder and more dread;
It reached the ship, it split the bay:
The ship went down like lead.

" Stunned by that loud and dreadful sound,          550
Which sky and ocean smote,
Like one that hath been seven days drowned,
My body lay afloat;
But swift as dreams, myself I found
Within the Pilot's boat.          555

" Upon the whirl, where sank the ship,
The boat spun round and round;
And all was still, save that the hill
Was telling of the sound.

" I moved my lips — the Pilot shrieked,          560
And fell down in a fit;
The holy Hermit raised his eyes,
And prayed where he did sit.

" I took the oars: the Pilot's boy,
Who now doth crazy go,          565
Laughed loud and long, and all the while
His eyes went to and fro.
' Ha, ha!' quoth he, ' full plain I see
The Devil knows how to row.'

" And now, all in my own countree,          570
I stood on the firm land!
The Hermit stepped forth from the boat,
And scarcely he could stand.

" ' O shrieve me, shrieve me, holy man!'
The Hermit crossed his brow.          575
' Say quick,' quoth he, ' I bid thee say,
What manner of man art thou?'

"Forthwith this frame of mine was wrenched
With a woeful agony,
Which forced me to begin my tale;                          580
And then it left me free.


"Since then, at an uncertain hour,
That agony returns;
And till my ghastly tale is told,
This heart within me burns.                                585


"I pass, like night, from land to land;
I have strange power of speech;
That moment that his face I see,
I know the man that must hear me:
To him my tale I teach.                                    590


"What loud uproar bursts from that door!
The wedding guests are there;
But in the garden bower the bride
And bridemaids singing are:
And hark the little vesper bell,                           595
Which biddeth me to prayer!


"O Wedding Guest! this soul hath been
Alone on a wide, wide sea:
So lonely 'twas, that God himself
Scarce seemèd there to be.                                 600


"Oh, sweeter than the marriage feast,
'Tis sweeter far to me,
To walk together to the kirk
With a goodly company, —

" To walk together to the kirk,
And all together pray,
While each to his great Father bends, —
Old men, and babes, and loving friends,
And youths and maidens gay !                605

" Farewell, farewell ! but this I tell
To thee, thou Wedding Guest, —            610
He prayeth well who loveth well
Both man and bird and beast.

" He prayeth best who loveth best
All things, both great and small;
For the dear God who loveth us,           615
He made and loveth all."

The Mariner, whose eye is bright,
Whose beard with age is hoar,
Is gone : and now the Wedding Guest       620
Turned from the bridegroom's door.

He went like one that hath been stunned,
And is of sense forlorn :
A sadder and a wiser man
He rose the morrow morn.                   625

MATTHEW ARNOLD

SOHRAB AND RUSTUM.

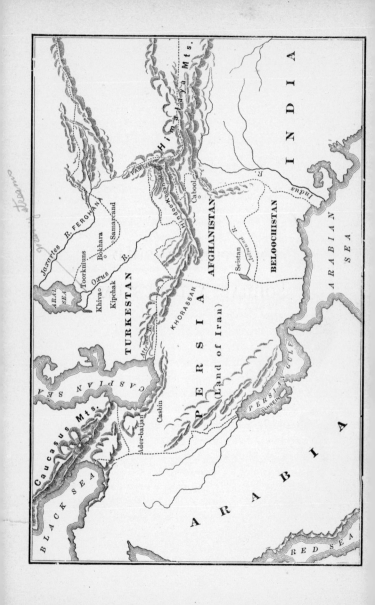

# SOHRAB AND RUSTUM.

## AN EPISODE.

*Oxus*

And the first gray of morning filled the east,
And the fog rose out of the Oxus stream.
But all the Tartar camp along the stream
Was hushed, and still the men were plunged in sleep.
Sohrab alone, he slept not; all night long          5
He had lain wakeful, tossing on his bed:
But when the gray dawn stole into his tent,
He rose, and clad himself, and girt his sword,
And took his horseman's cloak, and left his tent,
And went abroad into the cold wet fog,          10
Through the dim camp to Peran-Wisa's tent.
   Through the black Tartar tents he passed, which stood
Clustering like bee-hives on the low flat strand
Of Oxus, where the summer-floods o'erflow
When the sun melts the snows in high Pamere;          15
Through the black tents he passed, o'er that low strand,
And to a hillock came, a little back
From the stream's brink, — the spot where first a boat,
Crossing the stream in summer, scrapes the land.
The men of former times had crowned the top          20
With a clay fort; but that was fallen, and now
The Tartars built there Peran-Wisa's tent,
A dome of laths, and o'er it felts were spread.

And Sohrab came there, and went in, and stood
Upon the thick piled carpets in the tent,　　　　25
And found the old man sleeping on his bed
Of rugs and felts, and near him lay his arms.
And Peran-Wisa heard him, though the step
Was dulled; for he slept light, an old man's sleep;
And he rose quickly on one arm, and said, —　　　30
　"Who art thou? for it is not yet clear dawn.
Speak! is there news, or any night alarm?"
　But Sohrab came to the bedside, and said, —
"Thou know'st me, Peran-Wisa! it is I.
The sun has not yet risen, and the foe　　　　35
Sleep: but I sleep not; all night long I lie
Tossing and wakeful, and I come to thee.
For so did King Afrasiab bid me seek
Thy counsel, and to heed thee as thy son,
In Samarcand, before the army marched;　　　40
And I will tell thee what my heart desires.
Thou know'st if, since from Ader-baijan first
I came among the Tartars, and bore arms,
I have still served Afrasiab well, and shown,
At my boy's years, the courage of a man.　　　45
This too thou know'st, that while I still bear on
The conquering Tartar ensigns through the world,
And beat the Persians back on every field,
I seek one man, one man, and one alone, —
Rustum, my father; who I hoped should greet,　　　50
Should one day greet, upon some well-fought field,
His not unworthy, not inglorious son.
So I long hoped, but him I never find.
Come then, hear now, and grant me what I ask.
Let the two armies rest to-day; but I　　　　55
Will challenge forth the bravest Persian lords

To meet me, man to man : if I prevail,
Rustum will surely hear it ; if I fall —
Old man, the dead need no one, claim no kin.
Dim is the rumor of a common fight,                               60
Where host meets host, and many names are sunk ;
But of a single combat fame speaks clear."
  He spoke ; and Peran-Wisa took the hand
Of the young man in his, and sighed, and said, —
"O Sohrab, an unquiet heart is thine !                            65
Canst thou not rest among the Tartar chiefs,
And share the battle's common chance with us
Who love thee, but must press forever first,
In single fight incurring single risk,
To find a father thou hast never seen ?                           70
That were far best, my son, to stay with us
Unmurmuring ; in our tents, while it is war,
And when 'tis truce, then in Afrasiab's towns.
But if this one desire indeed rules all,
To seek out Rustum — seek him not through fight !                 75
Seek him in peace, and carry to his arms,
O Sohrab, carry an unwounded son !
But far hence seek him, for he is not here.
For now it is not as when I was young,
When Rustum was in front of every fray :                          80
But now he keeps apart, and sits at home,
In Seistan, with Zal, his father old ;
Whether that his own mighty strength at last
Feels the abhorred approaches of old age ;
Or in some quarrel with the Persian king.                         85
There go ! — Thou wilt not ?  Yet my heart forebodes
Danger or death awaits thee on this field.
Fain would I know thee safe and well, though lost
To us ; fain therefore send thee hence in peace

To seek thy father, not seek single fights 90
In vain. But who can keep the lion's cub
From ravening, and who govern Rustum's son?
Go, I will grant thee what thy heart desires."
   So said he, and dropped Sohrab's hand, and left
His bed, and the warm rugs whereon he lay; 95
And o'er his chilly limbs his woollen coat
He passed, and tied his sandals on his feet,
And threw a white cloak round him, and he took
In his right hand a ruler's staff, no sword;
And on his head he set his sheep-skin cap, 100
Black, glossy, curled, the fleece of Kara-Kul;
And raised the curtain of his tent, and called
His herald to his side, and went abroad.
   The sun by this had risen, and cleared the fog
From the broad Oxus and the glittering sands. 105
And from their tents the Tartar horseman filed
Into the open plain: so Haman bade, —
Haman, who next to Peran-Wisa ruled
The host, and still was in his lusty prime.
From their black tents, long files of horse, they streamed;
As when some gray November morn the files, 111
In marching order spread, of long-necked cranes
Stream over Casbin and the southern slopes
Of Elburz, from the Aralian estuaries,
Or some frore Caspian reed-bed, southward bound 115
For the warm Persian seaboard, — so they streamed.
The Tartars of the Oxus, the king's guard,
First, with black sheep-skin caps and with long spears;
Large men, large steeds, who from Bokhara came
And Khiva, and ferment the milk of mares, 120
Next, the more temperate Toorkmuns of the south,
The Tukas, and the lances of Salore,

And those from Attruck and the Caspian sands;
Light men and on light steeds, who only drink
The acrid milk of camels, and their wells.     **125**
And then a swarm of wandering horse, who came
From far, and a more doubtful service owned, —
The Tartars of Ferghana, from the banks
Of the Jaxartes, men with scanty beards
And close-set skull-caps; and those wilder hordes     **130**
Who roam o'er Kipchak and the northern waste,
Kalmucks and unkempt Kuzzaks, tribes who stray
Nearest the pole, and wandering Kirghizzes,
Who come on shaggy ponies from Pamere, —
These all filed out from camp into the plain.     **135**
And on the other side the Persians formed, —
First a light cloud of horse, Tartars they seemed,
The Ilyats of Khorassan; and behind,
The royal troops of Persia, horse and foot,
Marshalled battalions bright in burnished steel.     **140**
But Peran-Wisa with his herald came,
Threading the Tartar squadrons to the front,
And with his staff kept back the foremost ranks.
And when Ferood, who led the Persians, saw
That Peran-Wisa kept the Tartars back,     **145**
He took his spear, and to the front he came,
And checked his ranks, and fixed them where they stood.
And the old Tartar came upon the sand
Betwixt the silent hosts, and spake, and said, —
  "Ferood, and ye, Persians and Tartars, hear!     **150**
Let there be truce between the hosts to-day.
But choose a champion from the Persian lords
To fight our champion Sohrab, man to man."
  As in the country, on a morn in June,
When the dew glistens on the pearled ears,     **155**

D

A shiver runs through the deep corn for joy, —
So, when they heard what Peran-Wisa said,
A thrill through all the Tartar squadrons ran
Of pride and hope for Sohrab, whom they loved.

  But as a troop of pedlers from Cabool    160
Cross underneath the Indian Caucasus,
That vast sky-neighboring mountain of milk snow;
Crossing so high, that, as they mount, they pass
Long flocks of travelling birds dead on the snow,
Choked by the air, and scarce can they themselves  165
Slake their parched throats with sugared mulberries;
In single file they move, and stop their breath,
For fear they should dislodge the o'erhanging snows, —
So the pale Persians held their breath with fear.

  And to Ferood his brother chiefs came up   170
To counsel; Gudurz and Zoarrah came,
And Feraburz, who ruled the Persian host
Second, and was the uncle of the king;
These came and counselled, and then Gudurz said, —

  "Ferood, shame bids us take their challenge up,  175
Yet champion have we none to match this youth.
He has the wild stag's foot, the lion's heart.
But Rustum came last night; aloof he sits
And sullen, and has pitched his tents apart.
Him will I seek, and carry to his ear    180
The Tartar challenge, and this young man's name;
Haply he will forget his wrath, and fight.
Stand forth the while, and take their challenge up."

  So spake he; and Ferood stood forth and cried, —
"Old man, be it agreed as thou hast said!   185
Let Sohrab arm, and we will find a man."

  He spake; and Peran-Wisa turned, and strode
Back through the opening squadrons to his tent.

But through the anxious Persians Gudurz ran,
And crossed the camp which lay behind, and reached,   190
Out on the sands beyond it, Rustum's tents.
Of scarlet cloth they were, and glittering gay,
Just pitched; the high pavilion in the midst
Was Rustum's, and his men lay camped around.
And Gudurz entered Rustum's tent, and found   195
Rustum; his morning meal was done, but still
The table stood before him, charged with food, —
A side of roasted sheep, and cakes of bread,
And dark-green melons; and there Rustum sate
Listless, and held a falcon on his wrist,   200
And played with it; but Gudurz came and stood
Before him; and he looked, and saw him stand,
And with a cry sprang up, and dropped the bird,
And greeted Gudurz with both hands, and said, —

"Welcome! these eyes could see no better sight.   205
What news? but sit down first, and eat and drink."

But Gudurz stood in the tent-door, and said, —
"Not now. A time will come to eat and drink,
But not to-day: to-day has other needs.
The armies are drawn out, and stand at gaze;   210
For, from the Tartars is a challenge brought
To pick a champion from the Persian lords
To fight their champion — and thou know'st his name:
Sohrab men call him, but his birth is hid.
O Rustum, like thy might is this young man's!   215
He has the wild stag's foot, the lion's heart;
And he is young, and Iran's chiefs are old,
Or else too weak; and all eyes turn to thee.
Come down and help us, Rustum, or we lose!"

He spoke; but Rustum answered with a smile, —   220
"Go to! if Iran's chiefs are old, then I

Am older.　If the young are weak, the king
Errs strangely; for the king, for Kai Khosroo,
Himself is young, and honors younger men,
And lets the aged moulder to their graves.　　　　225
Rustum he loves no more, but loves the young:
The young may rise at Sohrab's vaunts, not I.
For what care I, though all speak Sohrab's fame?
For would that I myself had such a son,
And not that one slight helpless girl I have!　　　230
A son so famed, so brave, to send to war,
And I to tarry with the snow-haired Zal,
My father, whom the robber Afghans vex,
And clip his borders short, and drive his herds,
And he has none to guard his weak old age.　　　235
There would I go, and hang my armor up,
And with my great name fence that weak old man,
And spend the goodly treasures I have got,
And rest my age, and hear of Sohrab's fame,
And leave to death the hosts of thankless kings,　　　240
And with these slaughterous hands draw sword no more."

　　He spoke, and smiled; and Gudurz made reply, —
" What then, O Rustum, will men say to this,
When Sohrab dares our bravest forth, and seeks
Thee most of all, and thou, whom most he seeks,　　　245
Hidest thy face?　Take heed lest men should say, —
*Like some old miser, Rustum hoards his fame,*
*And shuns to peril it with younger men.*"

　　And, greatly moved, then Rustum made reply, —
" O Gudurz, wherefore dost thou say such word?　　　250
Thou knowest better words than this to say.
What is one more, one less, obscure or famed,
Valiant or craven, young or old, to me?
Are not they mortal? am not I myself?

But who for men of naught would do great deeds?    255
Come, thou shalt see how Rustum hoards his fame!
But I will fight unknown, and in plain arms:
Let not men say of Rustum, he was matched
In single fight with any mortal man."

He spoke, and frowned; and Gudurz turned, and ran    260
Back quickly through the camp in fear and joy, —
Fear at his wrath, but joy that Rustum came.
But Rustum strode to his tent-door, and called
His followers in, and bade them bring his arms,
And clad himself in steel.    The arms he chose    265
Were plain, and on his shield was no device;
Only his helm was rich, inlaid with gold,
And, from the fluted spine a-top, a plume
Of horse-hair waved, a scarlet horse-hair plume.
So armed, he issued forth; and Ruksh, his horse,    270
Followed him like a faithful hound at heel, —
Ruksh, whose renown was noised through all the earth,
The horse whom Rustum on a foray once
Did in Bokhara by the river find
A colt beneath its dam, and drove him home,    275
And reared him; a bright bay, with lofty crest,
Dight with a saddle-cloth of broidered green
Crusted with gold, and on the ground were worked
All beasts of chase, all beasts which hunters know.
So followed, Rustum left his tents, and crossed    280
The camp, and to the Persian host appeared.
And all the Persians knew him, and with shouts
Hailed; but the Tartars knew not who he was.
And dear as the wet diver to the eyes
Of his pale wife who waits and weeps on shore,    285
By sandy Bahrein, in the Persian Gulf,
Plunging all day in the blue waves, at night,

Having made up his tale of precious pearls
Rejoins her in their hut upon the sands, —
So dear to the pale Persians Rustum came.                    290
    And Rustum to the Persian front advanced;
And Sohrab armed in Haman's tent, and came.
And as a-field the reapers cut a swath
Down through the middle of a rich man's corn,
And on each side are squares of standing corn,              295
And in the midst a stubble short and bare, —
So on each side were squares of men, with spears
Bristling, and in the midst the open sand.
And Rustum came upon the sand, and cast
His eyes toward the Tartar tents, and saw                   300
Sohrab come forth, and eyed him as he came.
    As some rich woman, on a winter's morn,
Eyes through her silken curtains the poor drudge
Who with numb blackened fingers makes her fire, —
At cock-crow, on a starlit winter's morn,                  305
When the frost flowers the whitened window-panes, —
And wonders how she lives, and what the thoughts
Of that poor drudge may be; so Rustum eyed
The unknown adventurous youth, who from afar
Came seeking Rustum, and defying forth                     310
All the most valiant chiefs; long he perused
His spirited air, and wondered who he was.
For very young he seemed, tenderly reared;
Like some young cypress, tall and dark and straight,
Which in a queen's secluded garden throws                  315
Its slight dark shadow on the moonlit turf,
By midnight, to a bubbling fountain's sound, —
So slender Sohrab seemed, so softly reared.
And a deep pity entered Rustum's soul
As he beheld him coming; and he stood,                     320

And beckoned to him with his hand; and said, —
"O thou young man, the air of heaven is soft,
And warm, and pleasant; but the grave is cold!
Heaven's air is better than the cold dead grave.
Behold me! I am vast, and clad in iron,                          325
And tried; and I have stood on many a field
Of blood, and I have fought with many a foe:
Never was that field lost, or that foe saved.
O Sohrab, wherefore wilt thou rush on death?
Be governed: quit the Tartar host, and come                      330
To Iran, and be as my son to me,
And fight beneath my banner till I die!
There are no youths in Iran brave as thou."
     So he spake, mildly. Sohrab heard his voice,
The mighty voice of Rustum, and he saw                           335
His giant figure planted on the sand,
Sole, like some single tower, which a chief
Hath builded on the waste in former years
Against the robbers; and he saw that head,
Streaked with its first gray hairs; hope filled his soul,        340
And he ran forward, and embraced his knees,
And clasped his hand within his own, and said, —
     "Oh, by thy father's head! by thine own soul!
Art thou not Rustum? Speak! art thou not he?"
     But Rustum eyed askance the kneeling youth,                 345
And turned away, and spake to his own soul, —
     "Ah me! I muse what this young fox may mean!
False, wily, boastful, are these Tartar boys.
For if I now confess this thing he asks,
And hide it not, but say, *Rustum is here!*                      350
He will not yield indeed, nor quit our foes;
But he will find some pretext not to fight,
And praise my fame, and proffer courteous gifts,

A belt or sword perhaps, and go his way.
And on a feast-tide, in Afrasiab's hall                    355
In Samarcand, he will arise and cry, —
   'I challenged once, when the two armies camped
Beside the Oxus, all the Persian lords
To cope with me in single fight; but they
Shrank, only Rustum dared; then he and I          360
Changed gifts, and went on equal terms away.'
So will he speak, perhaps, while men applaud;
Then were the chiefs of Iran shamed through me."
   And then he turned, and sternly spake aloud, —
"Rise! wherefore dost thou vainly question thus      365
Of Rustum?  I am here, whom thou hast called
By challenge forth; make good thy vaunt, or yield!
Is it with Rustum only thou wouldst fight?
Rash boy, men look on Rustum's face, and flee!
For well I know, that did great Rustum stand        370
Before thy face this day, and were revealed,
There would be then no talk of fighting more.
But being what I am, I tell thee this, —
Do thou record it in thine inmost soul:
Either thou shalt renounce thy vaunt, and yield,      375
Or else thy bones shall strew this sand, till winds
Bleach them, or Oxus with his summer-floods,
Oxus in summer wash them all away."
   He spoke; and Sohrab answered, on his feet, —
"Art thou so fierce?  Thou wilt not fright me so!      380
I am no girl, to be made pale by words.
Yet this thou hast said well, did Rustum stand
Here on this field, there were no fighting then.
But Rustum is far hence, and we stand here.
Begin! thou art more vast, more dread than I;      385
And thou art proved, I know, and I am young —

But yet success sways with the breath of Heaven.
And though thou thinkest that thou knowest sure
Thy victory, yet thou canst not surely know.
For we are all, like swimmers in the sea,     390
Poised on the top of a huge wave of fate,
Which hangs uncertain to which side to fall;
And whether it will heave us up to land,
Or whether it will roll us out to sea, —
Back out to sea, to the deep waves of death, —     395
We know not, and no search will make us know:
Only the event will teach us in its hour."

　　He spoke; and Rustum answered not, but hurled
His spear: down from the shoulder, down it came,
As on some partridge in the corn a hawk,     400
That long has towered in the airy clouds,
Drops like a plummet; Sohrab saw it come,
And sprang aside, quick as a flash; the spear
Hissed, and went quivering down into the sand,
Which it sent flying wide.　Then Sohrab threw     405
In turn, and full struck Rustum's shield; sharp rang,
The iron plates rang sharp, but turned the spear.
And Rustum seized his club, which none but he
Could wield; an unlopped trunk it was, and huge,
Still rough, — like those which men in treeless plains     410
To build them boats fish from the flooded rivers,
Hyphasis or Hydaspes, when, high up
By their dark springs, the wind in winter-time
Hath made in Himalayan forests wrack,
And strewn the channels with torn boughs, — so huge     415
The club which Rustum lifted now, and struck
One stroke; but again Sohrab sprang aside,
Lithe as the glancing snake, and the club came
Thundering to earth, and leapt from Rustum's hand.

And Rustum followed his own blow, and fell       420
To his knees, and with his fingers clutched the sand.
And now might Sohrab have unsheathed his sword,
And pierced the mighty Rustum while he lay
Dizzy, and on his knees, and choked with sand;
But he looked on, and smiled, nor bared his sword,    425
But courteously drew back, and spoke, and said, —
    "Thou strik'st too hard! that club of thine will float
Upon the summer-floods, and not my bones.
But rise, and be not wroth! not wroth am I;
No, when I see thee, wrath forsakes my soul.    430
Thou say'st thou art not Rustum; be it so!
Who art thou, then, that canst so touch my soul?
Boy as I am, I have seen battles too, —
Have waded foremost in their bloody waves,
And heard their hollow roar of dying men;    435
But never was my heart thus touched before.
Are they from Heaven, these softenings of the heart?
O thou old warrior, let us yield to Heaven!
Come, plant we here in earth our angry spears,
And make a truce, and sit upon this sand,    440
And pledge each other in red wine, like friends,
And thou shalt talk to me of Rustum's deeds.
There are enough foes in the Persian host,
Whom I may meet, and strike, and feel no pang;
Champions enough Afrasiab has, whom thou    445
Mayst fight; fight *them*, when they confront thy spear!
But oh, let there be peace 'twixt thee and me!"
    He ceased; but while he spake, Rustum had risen,
And stood erect, trembling with rage; his club
He left to lie, but had regained his spear,    450
Whose fiery point now in his mailed right hand
Blazed bright and baleful, like that autumn-star,

The baleful sign of fevers; dust had soiled
His stately crest, and dimmed his glittering arms.
His breast heaved, his lips foamed, and twice his voice   455
Was choked with rage; at last these words broke way: —
  "Girl! nimble with thy feet, not with thy hands!
Curled minion, dancer, coiner of sweet words!
Fight, let me hear thy hateful voice no more!
Thou art not in Afrasiab's garden now   460
With Tartar girls, with whom thou art wont to dance;
But on the Oxus-sands, and in the dance
Of battle, and with me, who make no play
Of war: I fight it out, and hand to hand.
Speak not to me of truce, and pledge, and wine!   465
Remember all thy valor; try thy feints
And cunning! all the pity I had is gone,
Because thou hast shamed me before both the hosts
With thy light skipping tricks and thy girl's wiles."
  He spoke; and Sohrab kindled at his taunts,   470
And he too drew his sword; at once they rushed
Together, as two eagles on one prey
Come rushing down together from the clouds,
One from the east, one from the west; their shields
Dashed with a clang together, and a din   475
Rose, such as that the sinewy woodcutters
Make often in the forest's heart at morn,
Of hewing axes, crashing trees, — such blows
Rustum and Sohrab on each other hailed.
And you would say that sun and stars took part   480
In that unnatural conflict: for a cloud
Grew suddenly in heaven, and darked the sun
Over the fighters' heads; and a wind rose
Under their feet, and moaning swept the plain,
And in a sandy whirlwind wrapped the pair.   485

In gloom they twain were wrapped, and they alone;
For both the on-looking hosts on either hand
Stood in broad daylight, and the sky was pure,
And the sun sparkled on the Oxus stream.
But in the gloom they fought, with bloodshot eyes          490
And laboring breath.   First Rustum struck the shield
Which Sohrab held stiff out; the steel-piked spear
Rent the tough plates, but failed to reach the skin,
And Rustum plucked it back with angry groan.
Then Sohrab with his sword smote Rustum's helm,           495
Nor clove its steel quite through; but all the crest
He shore away, and that proud horse-hair plume,
Never till now defiled, sank to the dust;
And Rustum bowed his head.   But then the gloom
Grew blacker, thunder rumbled in the air                 500
And lightnings rent the cloud; and Ruksh the horse,
Who stood at hand, uttered a dreadful cry:
No horse's cry was that, most like the roar
Of some pained desert-lion, who all day
Has trailed the hunter's javelin in his side,            505
And comes at night to die upon the sand;
The two hosts heard that cry, and quaked for fear,
And Oxus curdled as it crossed his stream.
But Sohrab heard, and quailed not, but rushed on,
And struck again; and again Rustum bowed                 510
His head; but this time all the blade, like glass,
Sprang in a thousand shivers on the helm,
And in the hand the hilt remained alone.
Then Rustum raised his head; his dreadful eyes
Glared, and he shook on high his menacing spear,         515
And shouted, *Rustum!*  Sohrab heard that shout,
And shrank amazed: back he recoiled one step,
And scanned with blinking eyes the advancing form:

And then he stood bewildered, and he dropped
His covering shield, and the spear pierced his side. 520
He reeled, and staggering back sank to the ground.
And then the gloom dispersed, and the wind fell,
And the bright sun broke forth, and melted all
The cloud; and the two armies saw the pair, —
Saw Rustum standing safe upon his feet, 525
And Sohrab wounded on the bloody sand.
　Then, with a bitter smile, Rustum began, -
"Sohrab, thou thoughtest in thy mind to kill
A Persian lord this day, and strip his corpse,
And bear thy trophies to Afrasiab's tent; 530
Or else that the great Rustum would come down
Himself to fight, and that thy wiles would move
His heart to take a gift, and let thee go.
And then that all the Tartar host would praise
Thy courage or thy craft, and spread thy fame, 535
To glad thy father in his weak old age.
Fool, thou art slain, and by an unknown man!
Dearer to the red jackals shalt thou be
Than to thy friends, and to thy father old."
　And, with a fearless mien, Sohrab replied, — 540
"Unknown thou art, yet thy fierce vaunt is vain.
Thou dost not slay me, proud and boastful man!
No! Rustum slays me, and this filial heart.
For, were I matched with ten such men as thee,
And I were that which till to-day I was, 545
They should be lying here, I standing there.
But that belovèd name unnerved my arm, —
That name, and something, I confess, in thee,
Which troubles all my heart, and made my shield
Fall; and thy spear transfixed an unarmed foe. 550
And now thou boastest, and insult'st my fate.

But hear thou this, fierce man, tremble to hear:
The mighty Rustum shall avenge my death!
My father, whom I seek through all the world,
He shall avenge my death, and punish thee!"          555
    As when some hunter in the spring hath found
A breeding eagle sitting on her nest,
Upon the craggy isle of a hill-lake,
And pierced her with an arrow as she rose,
And followed her to find her where she fell          560
Far off; anon her mate comes winging back
From hunting, and a great way off descries
His huddling young left sole; at that, he checks
His pinion, and with short uneasy sweeps
Circles above his eyry, with loud screams          565
Chiding his mate back to her nest; but she
Lies dying, with the arrow in her side,
In some far stony gorge out of his ken,
A heap of fluttering feathers, — never more
Shall the lake glass her, flying over it;          570
Never the black and dripping precipices
Echo her stormy scream as she sails by, —
As that poor bird flies home, nor knows his loss,
So Rustum knew not his own loss, but stood
Over his dying son, and knew him not.          575
    And with a cold, incredulous voice, he said, —
" What prate is this of fathers and revenge ?
The mighty Rustum never had a son."
    And, with a failing voice, Sohrab replied, —
" Ah, yes, he had! and that lost son am I.          580
Surely the news will one day reach his ear, —
Reach Rustum, where he sits, and tarries long,
Somewhere, I know not where, but far from here;
And pierce him like a stab, and make him leap

To arms, and cry for vengeance upon thee.     585
Fierce man, bethink thee, for an only son!
What will that grief, what will that vengeance, be?
Oh, could I live till I that grief had seen!
Yet him I pity not so much, but her,
My mother, who in Ader-baijan dwells     590
With that old king, her father, who grows gray
With age, and rules over the valiant Koords.
Her most I pity, who no more will see
Sohrab returning from the Tartar camp,
With spoils and honor, when the war is done.     595
But a dark rumor will be bruited up,
From tribe to tribe, until it reach her ear;
And then will that defenceless woman learn
That Sohrab will rejoice her sight no more·
But that in battle with a nameless foe,     600
By the far-distant Oxus, he is slain."
    He spoke; and as he ceased, he wept aloud,
Thinking of her he left, and his own death.
He spoke; but Rustum listened, plunged in thought.
Nor did he yet believe it was his son     605
Who spoke, although he called back names he knew;
For he had had sure tidings that the babe
Which was in Ader-baijan born to him
Had been a puny girl, no boy at all —
So that sad mother sent him word, for fear     610
Rustum should seek the boy, to train in arms.
And so he deemed that either Sohrab took,
By a false boast, the style of Rustum's son;
Or that men gave it him, to swell his fame.
So deemed he: yet he listened, plunged in thought;     615
And his soul set to grief, as the vast tide
Of the bright rocking ocean sets to shore

At the full moon; tears gathered in his eyes;
For he remembered his own early youth,
And all its bounding rapture; as, at dawn,                    620
The shepherd from his mountain-lodge descries
A far, bright city, smitten by the sun,
Through many rolling clouds, — so Rustum saw
His youth; saw Sohrab's mother in her bloom;
And that old king, her father, who loved well               625
His wandering guest, and gave him his fair child
With joy; and all the pleasant life they led,
They three, in that long-distant summer-time, —
The castle, and the dewy woods, and hunt
And hound, and morn on those delightful hills                630
In Ader-baijan.  And he saw that youth,
Of age and looks to be his own dear son,
Piteous and lovely, lying on the sand;
Like some rich hyacinth which by the scythe
Of an unskilful gardener has been cut,                       635
Mowing the garden grass-plots near its bed,
And lies, a fragrant tower of purple bloom,
On the mown, dying grass, — so Sohrab lay,
Lovely in death, upon the common sand.
And Rustum gazed on him with grief, and said, —             640
   "O Sohrab, thou indeed art such a son
Whom Rustum, wert thou his, might well have loved!
Yet here thou errest, Sohrab, or else men
Have told thee false: thou art not Rustum's son.
For Rustum had no son: one child he had, —                   645
But one, — a girl; who with her mother now
Plies some light female task, nor dreams of us, —
Of us she dreams not, nor of wounds, nor war."
   But Sohrab answered him in wrath; for now
The anguish of the deep-fixed spear grew fierce,             650

And he desired to draw forth the steel,
And let the blood flow free, and so to die.
But first he would convince his stubborn foe;
And, rising sternly on one arm, he said, —
"Man, who art thou who dost deny my words?  655
Truth sits upon the lips of dying men;
And falsehood, while I lived, was far from mine.
I tell thee, pricked upon this arm I bear
That seal which Rustum to my mother gave,
That she might prick it on the babe she bore."  660
He spoke; and all the blood left Rustum's cheeks,
And his knees tottered, and he smote his hand
Against his breast, his heavy mailèd hand,
That the hard iron corslet clanked aloud;
And to his heart he pressed the other hand,  665
And in a hollow voice he spake, and said, —
"Sohrab, that were a proof which could not lie!
If thou show this, then art thou Rustum's son."
Then, with weak hasty fingers, Sohrab loosed
His belt, and near the shoulder bared his arm,  670
And showed a sign in faint vermilion points
Pricked; as a cunning workman, in Pekin,
Pricks with vermilion some clear porcelain vase,
An emperor's gift, — at early morn he paints,
And all day long, and, when night comes, the lamp  675
Lights up his studious forehead and thin hands, —
So delicately pricked the sign appeared
On Sohrab's arm, the sign of Rustum's seal.
It was that griffin which of old reared Zal,
Rustum's great father, whom they left to die,  680
A helpless babe, among the mountain rocks;
Him that kind creature found, and reared, and loved;
Then Rustum took it for his glorious sign.

E

And Sohrab bared that image on his arm,
And himself scanned it long with mournful eyes,          685
And then he touched it with his hand, and said, —
    "How say'st thou?   Is that sign the proper sign
Of Rustum's son, or of some other man's?"
    He spoke; but Rustum gazed, and gazed, and stood
Speechless; and then he uttered one sharp cry, —          690
*O boy — thy father!* and his voice choked there.
And then a dark cloud passed before his eyes,
And his head swam, and he sank down to earth.
But Sohrab crawled to where he lay, and cast
His arms about his neck, and kissed his lips,          695
And with fond faltering fingers stroked his cheeks,
Trying to call him back to life; and life
Came back to Rustum, and he oped his eyes,
And they stood wide with horror; and he seized
In both his hands the dust which lay around,          700
And threw it on his head, and smirched his hair, —
His hair, and face, and beard, and glittering arms;
And strong convulsive groanings shook his breast,
And his sobs choked him; and he clutched his sword,
To draw it, and forever let life out.          705
But Sohrab saw his thought, and held his hands,
And with a soothing voice he spake, and said, —
    "Father, forbear! for I but meet to-day
The doom which at my birth was written down
In Heaven, and thou art Heaven's unconscious hand.          710
Surely my heart cried out that it was thou,
When first I saw thee; and thy heart spoke too,
I know it! But fate trod those promptings down
Under its iron heel; fate, fate engaged
The strife, and hurled me on my father's spear.          715
But let us speak no more of this.   I find

My father, let me feel that I have found!
Come, sit beside me on this sand, and take
My head betwixt thy hands, and kiss my cheeks,
And wash them with thy tears, and say, *My son!*          720
Quick, quick! for numbered are my sands of life,
And swift; for like the lightning to this field
I came, and like the wind I go away,—
Sudden, and swift, and like a passing wind;
But it was writ in Heaven that this should be."          725
    So said he; and his voice released the heart
Of Rustum, and his tears broke forth; he cast
His arms round his son's neck, and wept aloud,
And kissed him.  And awe fell on both the hosts,
When they saw Rustum's grief; and Ruksh, the horse,      730
With his head bowing to the ground, and mane
Sweeping the dust, came near, and in mute woe
First to the one, then to the other, moved
His head, as if inquiring what their grief
Might mean; and from his dark, compassionate eyes,       735
The big warm tears rolled down, and caked the sand.
But Rustum chid him with stern voice, and said,—
    "Ruksh, now thou grievest; but, O Ruksh, thy feet
Should then have rotted on their nimble joints,
When first they bore thy master to this field!"          740
    But Sohrab looked upon the horse, and said,—
"Is this, then, Ruksh?  How often, in past days,
My mother told me of thee, thou brave steed,
My terrible father's terrible horse! and said,
That I should one day find thy lord and thee.            745
Come, let me lay my hand upon thy mane!
O Ruksh, thou art more fortunate than I!
For thou hast gone where I shall never go,
And snuffed the breezes of my father's home.

And thou hast trod the sands of Seistan,                    750
And seen the River of Helmund, and the Lake
Of Zirrah; and the agèd Zal himself
Has often stroked thy neck, and given thee food,
Corn in a golden platter, soaked with wine,
And said, *O Ruksh! bear Rustum well!*   But I            755
Have never known my grandsire's furrowed face,
Nor seen his lofty house in Seistan,
Nor slaked my thirst at the clear Helmund stream,
But lodged among my father's foes, and seen
Afrasiab's cities only, Samarcand,                         760
Bokhara, and lone Khiva in the waste,
And the black Toorkmun tents; and only drunk
The desert rivers, Moorghab and Tejend,
Kohik, and where the Kalmuks feed their sheep,
The northern Sir; and this great Oxus stream,             765
The yellow Oxus, by whose brink I die."
   Then, with a heavy groan, Rustum bewailed, —
"Oh that its waves were flowing over me!
Oh that I saw its grains of yellow silt
Roll tumbling in the current o'er my head!"               770
   But, with a grave mild voice, Sohrab replied, —
"Desire not that, my father! thou must live.
For some are born to do great deeds, and live .
As some are born to be obscured, and die.
Do thou the deeds I die too young to do,                  775
And reap a second glory in thine age;
Thou art my father, and thy gain is mine.
But come! thou seest this great host of men
Which follow me; I pray thee, slay not these!
Let me entreat for them: what have they done?            780
They followed me, my hope, my fame, my star.
Let them all cross the Oxus back in peace.

But me thou must bear hence, not send with them,
But carry me with thee to Seistan,
And place me on a bed, and mourn for me, — 785
Thou, and the snow-haired Zal, and all thy friends.
And thou must lay me in that lovely earth,
And heap a stately mound above my bones,
And plant a far-seen pillar over all;
That so the passing horseman on the waste 790
May see my tomb a great way off, and cry, —
*Sohrab, the mighty Rustum's son, lies there,*
*Whom his great father did in ignorance kill!*
And I be not forgotten in my grave."
·And with a mournful voice, Rustum replied, — 795
"Fear not! as thou hast said, Sohrab my son,
So shall it be; for I will burn my tents,
And quit the host, and bear thee hence with me,
And carry thee away to Seistan,
And place thee on a bed, and mourn for thee, 800
With the snow-headed Zal, and all my friends.
And I will lay thee in that lovely earth,
And heap a stately mound above thy bones,
And plant a far-seen pillar over all,
And men shall not forget thee in thy grave. 805
And I will spare thy host; yea, let them go!
Let them all cross the Oxus back in peace!
What should I do with slaying any more?
For would that all whom I have ever slain
Might be once more alive, — my bitterest foes, 810
And they who were called champions in their time,
And through whose death I won that fame I have, —
And I were nothing but a common man,
A poor, mean soldier, and without renown,
So thou mightest live too, my son, my son! 815

Or rather would that I, even I myself,
Might now be lying on this bloody sand,
Near death, and by an ignorant stroke of thine,
Not thou of mine! and I might die, not thou;
And I, not thou, be borne to Seistan;                    820
And Zal might weep above my grave, not thine;
And say, *O son, I weep thee not too sore,*
*For willingly, I know, thou met'st thine end !*
But now in blood and battles was my youth,
And full of blood and battles is my age,                 825
And I shall never end this life of blood."

  Then, at the point of death, Sohrab replied, —
" A life of blood indeed, thou dreadful man!
But thou shalt yet have peace; only not now,
Not yet! but thou shalt have it on that day,             830
When thou shalt sail in a high-masted ship,
Thou and the other peers of Kai Khosroo,
Returning home over the salt blue sea,
From laying thy dear master in his grave."

  And Rustum gazed in Sohrab's face, and said, —         835
" Soon be that day, my son, and deep that sea!
Till then, if fate so wills, let me endure."

  He spoke; and Sohrab smiled on him, and took
The spear, and drew it from his side, and eased
His wound's imperious anguish; but the blood             840
Came welling from the open gash, and life
Flowed with the stream; all down his cold white side
The crimson torrent ran, dim now and soiled,
Like the soiled tissue of white violets
Left, freshly gathered, on their native bank,            845
By children whom their nurses call with haste
In-doors from the sun's eye; his head drooped low,
His limbs grew slack; motionless, white, he lay, —

White, with eyes closed; only when heavy gasps,
Deep heavy gasps quivering through all his frame,     850
Convulsed him back to life, he opened them,
And fixed them feebly on his father's face;
Till now all strength was ebbed, and from his limbs
Unwillingly the spirit fled away,
Regretting the warm mansion which it left,     855
And youth, and bloom, and this delightful world.

So, on the bloody sand, Sohrab lay dead;
And the great Rustum drew his horseman's cloak
Down o'er his face, and sate by his dead son.
As those black granite pillars, once high-reared     860
By Jemshid in Persepolis, to bear
His house, now 'mid their broken flights of steps
Lie prone, enormous, down the mountain side, —
So in the sand lay Rustum by his son.

And night came down over the solemn waste,     865
And the two gazing hosts, and that sole pair,
And darkened all; and a cold fog, with night,
Crept from the Oxus. Soon a hum arose,
As of a great assembly loosed, and fires
Began to twinkle through the fog; for now     870
Both armies moved to camp, and took their meal;
The Persians took it on the open sands
Southward, the Tartars by the river-marge;
And Rustum and his son were left alone.

But the majestic river floated on,     *oxus*    875
Out of the mist and hum of that low land,
Into the frosty starlight, and there moved,
Rejoicing, through the hushed Chorasmian waste,
Under the solitary moon; *north* he flowed
Right for the polar star, past Orgunjè,     880
Brimming, and bright, and large; then sands begin

*Little force, so separates*

To hem his watery march, and dam his streams,
And split his currents; that for many a league
The shorn and parcelled Oxus strains along
Through beds of sand and matted rushy isles, —          885
Oxus, forgetting the bright speed he had
In his high mountain cradle in Pamere,
A foiled circuitous wanderer, — till at last
The longed-for dash of waves is heard, and wide
His luminous home of waters opens, bright          890
And tranquil, from whose floor the new-bathed stars
Emerge, and shine upon the Aral Sea.

# ALFRED, LORD TENNYSON

## ENOCH ARDEN

# ENOCH ARDEN.

———•◦•———

Long lines of cliff breaking have left a chasm;
And in the chasm are foam and yellow sands;
Beyond, red roofs about a narrow wharf
In cluster; then a moulder'd church; and higher
A long street climbs to one tall-tower'd mill;     5
And high in heaven behind it a gray down
With Danish barrows; and a hazelwood,
By autumn nutters haunted, flourishes
Green in a cuplike hollow of the down.

Here on this beach a hundred years ago,     10
Three children of three houses, Annie Lee,
The prettiest little damsel in the port,
And Philip Ray the miller's only son,
And Enoch Arden, a rough sailor's lad
Made orphan by a winter shipwreck, play'd     15
Among the waste and lumber of the shore,
Hard coils of cordage, swarthy fishing-nets,
Anchors of rusty fluke, and boats updrawn;
And built their castles of dissolving sand
To watch them overflow'd, or following up     20
And flying the white breaker, daily left
The little footprint daily wash'd away.

A narrow cave ran in beneath the cliff:
In this the children play'd at keeping house.
Enoch was host one day, Philip the next,                    25
While Annie still was mistress; but at times
Enoch would hold possession for a week:
'This is my house and this my little wife."
'Mine too" said Philip "turn and turn about:"
When, if they quarrell'd, Enoch stronger-made           30
Was master: then would Philip, his blue eyes
All flooded with the helpless wrath of tears,
Shriek out "I hate you, Enoch," and at this
The little wife would weep for company,
And pray them not to quarrel for her sake,               35
And say she would be little wife to both.

But when the dawn of rosy childhood past,
And the new warmth of life's ascending sun
Was felt by either, either fixed his heart
On that one girl; and Enoch spoke his love,              40
But Philip loved in silence; and the girl
Seem'd kinder unto Philip than to him;
But she loved Enoch; tho' she knew it not,
And would if ask'd deny it.   Enoch set
A purpose evermore before his eyes,                      45
To hoard all savings to the uttermost,
To purchase his own boat, and make a home
For Annie: and so prosper'd that at last
A luckier or a bolder fisherman,
A carefuller in peril, did not breathe                   50
For leagues along that breaker-beaten coast
Than Enoch.   Likewise had he served a year
On board a merchantman, and made himself
Full sailor; and he thrice had pluck'd a life

From the dread sweep of the down-streaming seas: 55
And all men look'd upon him favorably:
And ere he touch'd his one-and-twentieth May,
He purchased his own boat, and made a home
For Annie, neat and nestlike, halfway up
The narrow street that clamber'd toward the mill. 60

Then, on a golden autumn eventide,
The younger people making holiday,
With bag and sack and basket, great and small,
Went nutting to the hazels.   Philip stay'd
(His father lying sick and needing him) 65
An hour behind; but as he climb'd the hill,
Just where the prone edge of the wood began
To feather toward the hollow, saw the pair,
Enoch and Annie, sitting hand-in-hand,
His large gray eyes and weather-beaten face 70
All-kindled by a still and sacred fire,
That burn'd as on an altar.   Philip look'd,
And in their eyes and faces read his doom;
Then, as their faces drew together, groan'd,
And slipt aside, and like a wounded life 75
Crept down into the hollows of the wood;
There, while the rest were loud in merrymaking,
Had his dark hour unseen, and rose and past
Bearing a lifelong hunger in his heart.

So these were wed, and merrily rang the bells, 80
And merrily ran the years, seven happy years,
Seven happy years of health and competence,
And mutual love and honorable toil;
With children; first a daughter.   In him woke,
With his first babe's first cry, the noble wish 85

To save all earnings to the uttermost,
And give his child a better bringing-up
Than his had been, or hers; a wish renew'd,
When two years after came a boy to be
The rosy idol of her solitudes,                        90
While Enoch was abroad on wrathful seas,
Or often journeying landward; for in truth
Enoch's white horse, and Enoch's ocean-spoil
In ocean-smelling osier, and his face,
Rough-redden'd with a thousand winter gales,          95
Not only to the market-cross were known,
But in the leafy lanes behind the down,
Far as the portal-warding lion-whelp,
And peacock-yewtree of the lonely Hall,
Whose Friday fare was Enoch's ministering.           100

    Then came a change, as all things human change.
Ten miles to northward of the narrow port
Open'd a larger haven: thither used
Enoch at times to go by land or sea;
And once when there, and clambering on a mast        105
In harbor, by mischance he slipt and fell:
A limb was broken when they lifted him;
And while he lay recovering there, his wife
Bore him another son, a sickly one:
Another hand crept too across his trade              110
Taking her bread and theirs: and on him fell,
Altho' a grave and staid God-fearing man,
Yet lying thus inactive, doubt and gloom.
He seem'd, as in a nightmare of the night,
To see his children leading evermore                 115
Low miserable lives of hand-to-mouth,
And her, he loved, a beggar: then he pray'd

'Save them from this, whatever comes to me."
And while he pray'd, the master of that ship
Enoch had served in, hearing his mischance,      **120**
Came, for he knew the man and valued him,
Reporting of his vessel China-bound,
And wanting yet a boatswain.   Would he go?
There yet were many weeks before she sail'd,
Sail'd from this port.   Would Enoch have the place?
And Enoch all at once assented to it,            **126**
Rejoicing at that answer to his prayer.

So now that shadow of mischance appear'd
No graver than as when some little cloud
Cuts off the fiery highway of the sun,           **130**
And isles a light in the offing: yet the wife —
When he was gone — the children — what to do?
Then Enoch lay long-pondering on his plans;
To sell the boat — and yet he loved her well —
How many a rough sea had he weather'd in her!    **135**
He knew her, as a horseman knows his horse —
And yet to sell her — then with what she brought
Buy goods and stores — set Annie forth in trade
With all that seamen needed or their wives —
So might she keep the house while he was gone.   **140**
Should he not trade himself out yonder? go
This voyage more than once? yea twice or thrice
As oft as needed — last, returning rich,
Become the master of a larger craft,
With fuller profits lead an easier life,         **145**
Have all his pretty young ones educated,
And pass his days in peace among his own.

Thus Enoch in his heart determined all:
Then moving homeward came on Annie pale,

Nursing the sickly babe, her latest-born.          154
Forward she started with a happy cry,
And laid the feeble infant in his arms;
Whom Enoch took, and handled all his limbs,
Appraised his weight and fondled fatherlike,
But had no heart to break his purposes          155
To Annie, till the morrow, when he spoke.

Then first since Enoch's golden ring had girt
Her finger, Annie fought against his will:
Yet not with brawling opposition she,
But manifold entreaties, many a tear,          160
Many a sad kiss by day by night renew'd
(Sure that all evil would come out of it)
Besought him, supplicating, if he cared
For her or his dear children, not to go.
He not for his own self caring but her,          165
Her and her children, let her plead in vain;
So grieving held his will, and bore it thro'.

For Enoch parted with his old sea-friend,
Bought Annie goods and stores, and set his hand
To fit their little streetward sitting-room          170
With shelf and corner for the goods and stores
So all day long till Enoch's last at home,
Shaking their pretty cabin, hammer and axe,
Auger and saw, while Annie seem'd to hear
Her own death-scaffold raising, shrill'd and rang,          175
Till this was ended, and his careful hand, —
The space was narrow, — having order'd all
Almost as neat and close as Nature packs
Her blossom or her seedling, paused; and he,
Who needs would work for Annie to the last,          180
Ascending tired, heavily slept till morn.

And Enoch faced this morning of farewell
Brightly and boldly.   All his Annie's fears,
Save, as his Annie's, were a laughter to him.
Yet Enoch as a brave God-fearing man      185
Bow'd himself down, and in that mystery
Where God-in-man is one with man-in-God,
Pray'd for a blessing on his wife and babes
Whatever came to him: and then he said
"Annie, this voyage by the grace of God      190
Will bring fair weather yet to all of us.
Keep a clean hearth and a clear fire for me,
For I'll be back, my girl, before you know it."
Then lightly rocking baby's cradle "and he,
This pretty, puny, weakly little one, —      195
Nay — for I love him all the better for it —
God bless him, he shall sit upon my knees
And I will tell him tales of foreign parts,
And make him merry, when I come home again.
Come, Annie, come, cheer up before I go."      200

Him running on thus hopefully she heard,
And almost hoped herself; but when he turn'd
The current of his talk to graver things
In sailor fashion roughly sermonizing
On providence and trust in Heaven, she heard,      205
Heard and not heard him; as the village girl,
Who sets her pitcher underneath the spring,
Musing on him that used to fill it for her,
Hears and not hears, and lets it overflow.

At length she spoke "O Enoch, you are wise·      210
And yet for all your wisdom well know I
That I shall look upon your face no more."

F

"Well then," said Enoch "I shall look on yours.
Annie, the ship I sail in passes here
(He named the day); get you a seaman's glass,          215
Spy out my face, and laugh at all your fears."

But when the last of those last moments came,
" Annie, my girl, cheer up, be comforted,
Look to the babes, and till I come again
Keep everything shipshape, for I must go.          220
And fear no more for me; or if you fear
Cast all your cares on God; that anchor holds.
Is He not yonder in those uttermost
Parts of the morning? if I flee to these
Can I go from Him? and the sea is His,          225
The sea is His: He made it."

                              Enoch rose,
Cast his strong arms about his drooping wife,
And kiss'd his wonder-stricken little ones;
But for the third, the sickly one, who slept
After a night of feverous wakefulness,          230
When Annie would have raised him Enoch said
"Wake him not; let him sleep; how should the child
Remember this?" and kissed him in his cot.
But Annie from her baby's forehead clipt
A tiny curl, and gave it: this he kept          235
Thro' all his future; but now hastily caught
His bundle, waved his hand, and went his way.

She, when the day that Enoch mention'd, came,
Borrow'd a glass, but all in vain: perhaps
She could not fix the glass to suit her eye;          240
Perhaps her eye was dim, hand tremulous;

She saw him not: and while he stood on deck
Waving, the moment and the vessel past.

Ev'n to the last dip of the vanishing sail
She watch'd it, and departed weeping for him;  245
Then, tho' she mourn'd his absence as his grave,
Set her sad will no less to chime with his,
But throve not in her trade, not being bred
To barter, nor compensating the want
By shrewdness, neither capable of lies,  250
Nor asking overmuch and taking less,
And still foreboding " what would Enoch say ? "
For more than once, in days of difficulty
And pressure, had she sold her wares for less
Than what she gave in buying what she sold:  255
She fail'd and sadden'd knowing it; and thus,
Expectant of that news which never came,
Gain'd for her own a scanty sustenance,
And lived a life of silent melancholy.

Now the third child was sickly-born and grew  260
Yet sicklier, tho' the mother cared for it
With all a mother's care: nevertheless,
Whether her business often call'd her from it,
Or thro' the want of what it needed most,
Or means to pay the voice who best could tell  265
What most it needed — howso'e'er it was,
After a lingering, — ere she was aware, —
Like the caged bird escaping suddenly,
The little innocent soul flitted away.

In that same week when Annie buried it,  270
Philip's true heart, which hunger'd for her peace

(Since Enoch left he had not look'd upon her),
Smote him, as having kept aloof so long.
"Surely," said Philip, "I may see her now,
May be some little comfort;" therefore went,　　275
Past thro' the solitary room in front,
Paused for a moment at an inner door,
Then struck it thrice, and, no one opening,
Enter'd; but Annie, seated with her grief,
Fresh from the burial of her little one,　　280
Cared not to look on any human face,
But turn'd her own toward the wall and wept.
Then Philip standing up said falteringly
"Annie, I came to ask a favor of you."

He spoke; the passion in her moan'd reply　　285
"Favor from one so sad and so forlorn
As I am!" half abash'd him; yet unask'd,
His bashfulness and tenderness at war,
He set himself beside her, saying to her:

"I came to speak to you of what he wish'd,　　290
Enoch, your husband: I have ever said
You chose the best among us — a strong man:
For where he fixt his heart he set his hand
To do the thing he will'd, and bore it thro'.
And wherefore did he go this weary way,　　295
And leave you lonely? not to see the world —
For pleasure? — nay, but for the wherewithal
To give his babes a better bringing-up
Than his had been, or yours: that was his wish.
And if he come again, vext will he be　　300
To find the precious morning hours were lost.
And it would vex him even in his grave,

If he could know his babes were running wild
Like colts about the waste.   So, Annie, now —
Have we not known each other all our lives ?      305
I do beseech you by the love you bear
Him and his children not to say me nay —
For, if you will, when Enoch comes again
Why then he shall repay me — if you will,
Annie — for I am rich and well-to-do.      310
Now let me put the boy and girl to school :
This is the favor that I came to ask."

    Then Annie with her brows against the wall
Answer'd " I cannot look you in the face ;
I seem so foolish and so broken down.      315
When you came in, my sorrow broke me down ;
And now I think your kindness breaks me down ;
But Enoch lives ; that is borne in on me :
He will repay you : money can be repaid ;
Not kindness such as yours."

                And Philip ask'd      320
" Then you will let me, Annie ? "

                    There she turn'd,
She rose, and fixt her swimming eyes upon him,
And dwelt a moment on his kindly face,
Then calling down a blessing on his head
Caught at his hand, and wrung it passionately,      325
And past into the little garth beyond.
So lifted up in spirit he moved away.

    Then Philip put the boy and girl to school,
And bought them needful books, and every way,

Like one who does his duty by his own,     330
Made himself theirs; and tho' for Annie's sake,
Fearing the lazy gossip of the port,
He oft denied his heart his dearest wish,
And seldom crost her threshold, yet he sent
Gifts by the children, garden-herbs and fruit,     335
The late and early roses from his wall,
Or conies from the down, and now and then,
With some pretext of fineness in the meal
To save the offence of charitable, flour
From his tall mill that whistled on the waste.     340

But Philip did not fathom Annie's mind:
Scarce could the woman when he came upon her,
Out of full heart and boundless gratitude
Light on a broken word to thank him with.
But Philip was her children's all-in-all;     345
From distant corners of the street they ran
To greet his hearty welcome heartily;
Lords of his house and of his mill were they;
Worried his passive ear with petty wrongs
Or pleasures, hung upon him, play'd with him     350
And call'd him Father Philip. Philip gain'd
As Enoch lost; for Enoch seem'd to them
Uncertain as a vision or a dream,
Faint as a figure seen in early dawn
Down at the far end of an avenue,     355
Going we know not where: and so ten years,
Since Enoch left his hearth and native land,
Fled forward, and no news of Enoch came.

It chanced one evening Annie's children long'd
To go with others nutting to the wood,     360

And Annie would go with them; then they begg'd
For Father Philip (as they call'd him) too:
Him, like the working bee in blossom-dust,
Blanch'd with his mill, they found; and saying to him
" Come with us Father Philip" he denied;              365
But when the children pluck'd at him to go,
He laugh'd, and yielded readily to their wish,
For was not Annie with them? and they went.

    But after scaling half the weary down,
Just where the prone edge of the wood began       370
To feather toward the hollow, all her force
Fail'd her; and sighing, " Let me rest," she said:
So Philip rested with her well-content;
While all the younger ones with jubilant cries
Broke from their elders, and tumultuously           375
Down thro' the whitening hazels made a plunge
To the bottom, and dispersed, and bent or broke
The lithe reluctant boughs to tear away
Their tawny clusters, crying to each other
And calling, here and there, about the wood.        380

    But Philip sitting at her side forgot
Her presence, and remember'd one dark hour
Here in this wood, when like a wounded life
He crept into the shadow: at last he said,
Lifting his honest forehead, " Listen, Annie,      385
How merry they are down yonder in the wood.
Tired, Annie?" for she did not speak a word.
" Tired?" but her face had fall'n upon her hands;
At which, as with a kind of anger in him,
" The ship was lost," he said, " the ship was lost!   390
No more of that! why should you kill yourself

And make them orphans quite?" And Annie said
"I thought not of it: but — I know not why —
Their voices make me feel so solitary."

Then Philip coming somewhat closer spoke.   395
"Annie, there is a thing upon my mind,
And it has been upon my mind so long,
That tho' I know not when it first came there,
I know that it will out at last.  O Annie,
It is beyond all hope, against all chance,   400
That he who left you ten long years ago
Should still be living; well then — let me speak:
I grieve to see you poor and wanting help:
I cannot help you as I wish to do
Unless — they say that women are so quick —   405
Perhaps you know what I would have you know —
I wish you for my wife.  I fain would prove
A father to your children: I do think
They love me as a father: I am sure
That I love them as if they were mine own;   410
And I believe, if you were fast my wife,
That after all these sad uncertain years,
We might be still as happy as God grants
To any of his creatures.  Think upon it:
For I am well-to-do — no kin, no care,   415
No burthen, save my care for you and yours:
And we have known each other all our lives,
And I have loved you longer than you know."

Then answer'd Annie; tenderly she spoke:
"You have been as God's good angel in our house.   420
God bless you for it, God reward you for it,
Philip, with something happier than myself.

Can one love twice? can you be ever loved
As Enoch was? what is it that you ask?"
"I am content," he answer'd, "to be loved                      425
A little after Enoch."   "O," she cried,
Scared as it were, "dear Philip, wait a while:
If Enoch comes — but Enoch will not come —
Yet wait a year, a year is not so long:
Surely I shall be wiser in a year:                             430
O wait a little!"   Philip sadly said
"Annie, as I have waited all my life
I well may wait a little."   "Nay," she cried,
"I am bound: you have my promise — in a year:
Will you not bide your year as I bide mine?"                   435
And Philip answer'd "I will bide my year."

    Here both were mute, till Philip glancing up
Beheld the dead flame of the fallen day
Pass from the Danish barrow overhead;
Then fearing night and chill for Annie, rose                   440
And sent his voice beneath him thro' the wood.
Up came the children laden with their spoil;
Then all descended to the port, and there
At Annie's door he paused and gave his hand,
Saying gently "Annie, when I spoke to you,                     445
That was your hour of weakness.   I was wrong,
I am always bound to you, but you are free."
Then Annie weeping answer'd "I am bound."

    She spoke; and in one moment as it were,
While yet she went about her household ways,                   450
Ev'n as she dwelt upon his latest words,
That he had loved her longer than she knew,
That autumn into autumn flash'd again,

And there he stood once more before her face,
Claiming her promise.   "Is it a year?" she ask'd.   **455**
" Yes, if the nuts," he said, " be ripe again :
Come out and see."   But she — she put him off —
So much to look to — such a change — a month —
Give her a month — she knew that she was bound —
A month — no more.   Then Philip with his eyes   **460**
Full of that lifelong hunger, and his voice
Shaking a little like a drunkard's hand,
"Take your own time, Annie, take your own time."
And Annie could have wept for pity of him ;
And yet she held him on delayingly   **465**
With many a scarce-believable excuse,
Trying his truth and his long-sufferance,
Till half-another year had slipt away.

By this the lazy gossips of the port,
Abhorrent of a calculation crost,   **470**
Began to chafe as at a personal wrong.
Some thought that Philip did but trifle with her ;
Some that she but held off to draw him on ;
And others laugh'd at her and Philip too,
As simple folk that knew not their own minds,   **475**
And one, in whom all evil fancies clung
Like serpent eggs together, laughingly
Would hint at worse in either.   Her own son
Was silent, tho' he often look'd his wish ;
But evermore the daughter prest upon her   **480**
To wed the man so dear to all of them
And lift the household out of poverty ;
And Philip's rosy face contracting grew
Careworn and wan ; and all these things fell on her
Sharp as reproach.

At last one night it chanced 485
That Annie could not sleep, but earnestly
Pray'd for a sign "my Enoch, is he gone?"
Then compass'd round by the blind wall of night
Brook'd not the expectant terror of her heart,
Started from bed, and struck herself a light, 490
Then desperately seized the holy Book,
Suddenly set it wide to find a sign,
Suddenly put her finger on the text,
"Under the palm-tree." That was nothing to her:
No meaning there: she closed the Book and slept: 495
When lo! her Enoch sitting on a height,
Under a palm-tree, over him the Sun:
"He is gone," she thought, "he is happy, he is singing
Hosanna in the highest: yonder shines
The Sun of Righteousness, and these be palms 500
Whereof the happy people strowing cried
'Hosanna in the highest!'" Here she woke,
Resolved, sent for him and said wildly to him
"There is no reason why we should not wed."
"Then for God's sake," he answer'd, "both our sakes,
So you will wed me, let it be at once." 506

So these were wed and merrily rang the bells,
Merrily rang the bells and they were wed.
But never merrily beat Annie's heart.
A footstep seem'd to fall beside her path, 510
She knew not whence; a whisper on her ear,
She knew not what; nor loved she to be left
Alone at home, nor ventured out alone.
What ail'd her then, that ere she enter'd, often
Her hand dwelt lingeringly on the latch, 515
Fearing to enter: Philip thought he knew:

Such doubts and fears were common to her state,
Being with child: but when her child was born,
Then her new child was as herself renew'd,
Then the new mother came about her heart,                520
Then her good Philip was her all-in-all,
And that mysterious instinct wholly died.

And where was Enoch? prosperously sail'd
The ship "Good Fortune," tho' at setting forth
The Biscay, roughly riding eastward, shook               525
And almost overwhelm'd her, yet unvext
She slipt across the summer of the world,
Then after a long tumble about the Cape
And frequent interchange of foul and fair,
She passing thro' the summer world again,                530
The breath of heaven came continually
And sent her sweetly by the golden isles,
Till silent in her oriental haven.

There Enoch traded for himself, and bought
Quaint monsters for the market of those times,           535
A gilded dragon, also, for the babes.

Less lucky her home-voyage: at first indeed
Thro' many a fair sea-circle, day by day,
Scarce-rocking, her full-busted figure-head
Stared o'er the ripple feathering from her bows:         540
Then follow'd calms, and then winds variable,
Then baffling, a long course of them; and last
Storm, such as drove her under moonless heavens
Till hard upon the cry of "breakers" came
The crash of ruin, and the loss of all                   545
But Enoch and two others.   Half the night,

Buoy'd upon floating tackle and broken spars,
These drifted, stranding on an isle at morn
Rich, but the loneliest in a lonely sea.

    No want was there of human sustenance,       550
Soft fruitage, mighty nuts, and nourishing roots;
Nor save for pity was it hard to take
The helpless life so wild that it was tame.
There in a seaward-gazing mountain-gorge
They built, and thatch'd with leaves of palm, a hut, 555
Half hut, half native cavern.   So the three,
Set in this Eden of all plenteousness,
Dwelt with eternal summer, ill-content.

    For one, the youngest, hardly more than boy,
Hurt in that night of sudden ruin and wreck,    560
Lay lingering out a five-years' death-in-life.
They could not leave him.   After he was gone,
The two remaining found a fallen stem;
And Enoch's comrade, careless of himself,
Fire-hollowing this in Indian fashion, fell    565
Sun-stricken, and that other lived alone.
In those two deaths he read God's warning "wait."

    The mountain wooded to the peak, the lawns
And winding glades high up like ways to Heaven,
The slender coco's drooping crown of plumes,    570
The lightning flash of insect and of bird,
The lustre of the long convolvuluses
That coil'd around the stately stems, and ran
Ev'n to the limit of the land, the glows
And glories of the broad belt of the world,    575
All these he saw; but what he fain had seen

He could not see, the kindly human face,
Nor ever hear a kindly voice, but heard
The myriad shriek of wheeling ocean-fowl,
The league-long roller thundering on the reef,          58.
The moving whisper of huge trees that branch'd
And blossom'd in the zenith, or the sweep
Of some precipitous rivulet to the wave,
As down the shore he ranged, or all day long
Sat often in the seaward-gazing gorge,          58b
A shipwreck'd sailor, waiting for a sail:
No sail from day to day, but every day
The sunrise broken into scarlet shafts
Among the palms and ferns and precipices;
The blaze upon the waters to the east;          590
The blaze upon his island overhead;
The blaze upon the waters to the west;
Then the great stars that globed themselves in Heaven,
The hollower-bellowing ocean, and again
The scarlet shafts of sunrise — but no sail.          595

There often as he watch'd or seem'd to watch,
So still, the golden lizard on him paused,
A phantom made of many phantoms moved
Before him haunting him, or he himself
Moved haunting people, things and places, known          600
Far in a darker isle beyond the line;
The babes, their babble, Annie, the small house,
The climbing street, the mill, the leafy lanes,
The peacock-yewtree and the lonely Hall,
The horse he drove, the boat he sold, the chill          605
November dawns and dewy-glooming downs,
The gentle shower, the smell of dying leaves,
And the low moan of leaden-color'd seas.

Once likewise, in the ringing of his ears,
Tho' faintly, merrily — far and far away —    610
He heard the pealing of his parish bells;
Then, tho' he knew not wherefore, started up
Shuddering, and when the beauteous hateful isle
Return'd upon him, had not his poor heart
Spoken with That, which being everywhere    615
Lets none, who speaks with Him, seem all alone,
Surely the man had died of solitude.

Thus over Enoch's early-silvering head
The sunny and rainy seasons came and went
Year after year.  His hopes to see his own,    620
And pace the sacred old familiar fields,
Not yet had perish'd, when his lonely doom
Came suddenly to an end.  Another ship
(She wanted water) blown by baffling winds,
Like the Good Fortune, from her destined course,    625
Stay'd by this isle, not knowing where she lay:
For since the mate had seen at early dawn
Across a break on the mist-wreathen isle
The silent water slipping from the hills,
They sent a crew that landing burst away    630
In search of stream or fount, and fill'd the shores
With clamor.  Downward from his mountain-gorge
Stept the long-hair'd, long-bearded solitary,
Brown, looking hardly human, strangely clad,
Muttering and mumbling, idiotlike it seem'd,    635
With inarticulate rage, and making signs
They knew not what: and yet he led the way
To where the rivulets of sweet water ran;
And ever as he mingled with the crew,
And heard them talking, his long-bounden tongue    640

Was loosen'd, till he made them understand;
Whom, when their casks were fill'd they took aboard:
And there the tale he utter'd brokenly,
Scarce-credited at first but more and more,
Amazed and melted all who listen'd to it:                    645
And clothes they gave him and free passage home;
But oft he work'd among the rest and shook
His isolation from him.   None of these
Came from his country, or could answer him,
If question'd, aught of what he cared to know.               650
And dull the voyage was with long delays,
The vessel scarce sea-worthy; but evermore
His fancy fled before the lazy wind
Returning, till beneath a clouded moon
He like a lover down thro' all his blood                     355
Drew in the dewy meadowy morning-breath
Of England, blown across her ghostly wall;
And that same morning officers and men
Levied a kindly tax upon themselves,
Pitying the lonely man, and gave him it:                     660
Then moving up the coast they landed him,
Ev'n in that harbor whence he sail'd before.


There Enoch spoke no word to any one,
But homeward — home — what home? had he a home?
His home, he walk'd.   Bright was that afternoon,            665
Sunny but chill; till drawn thro' either chasm,
Where either haven open'd on the deeps,
Roll'd a sea-haze and whelm'd the world in gray;
Cut off the length of highway on before,
And left but narrow breadth to left and right               670
Of wither'd holt or tilth or pasturage.
On the nigh-naked tree the robin piped

Disconsolate, and thro' the dripping haze
The dead weight of the dead leaf bore it down.
Thicker the drizzle grew, deeper the gloom; 675
Last, as it seem'd, a great mist-blotted light
Flared on him, and he came upon the place.

Then down the long street having slowly stolen,
His heart foreshadowing all calamity,
His eyes upon the stones, he reach'd the home 680
Where Annie lived and loved him, and his babes
In those far-off seven happy years were born;
But finding neither light nor murmur there
(A bill of sale gleam'd thro' the drizzle) crept
Still downward thinking "dead or dead to me!" 685

Down to the pool and narrow wharf he went,
Seeking a tavern which of old he knew,
A front of timber-crost antiquity,
So propt, worm eaten, ruinously old,
He thought it must have gone; but he was gone 690
Who kept it; and his widow Miriam Lane,
With daily-dwindling profits held the house;
A haunt of brawling seamen once, but now
Stiller, with yet a bed for wandering men.
There Enoch rested silent many days. 695

But Miriam Lane was good and garrulous,
Nor let him be, but often breaking in,
Told him, with other annals of the port,
Not knowing — Enoch was so brown, so bow'd,
So broken — all the story of his house. 700
His baby's death, her growing poverty,
How Philip put her little ones to school,

G

And kept them in it, his long wooing her,
Her slow consent, and marriage, and the birth
Of Philip's child : and o'er his countenance        705
No shadow past, nor motion : any one,
Regarding, well had deem'd he felt the tale
Less than the teller : only when she closed
"Enoch, poor man, was cast away and lost"
He, shaking his gray head pathetically,              710
Repeated muttering "cast away and lost;"
Again in deeper inward whispers "lost!"

But Enoch yearn'd to see her face again;
"If I might look on her sweet face again
And know that she is happy." So the thought          715
Haunted and harass'd him, and drove him forth,
At evening when the dull November day
Was growing duller twilight, to the hill.
There he sat down gazing on all below;
There did a thousand memories roll upon him,         720
Unspeakable for sadness. By and by
The ruddy square of comfortable light,
Far-blazing from the rear of Philip's house,
Allured him, as the beacon-blaze allures
The bird of passage, till he madly strikes           725
Against it, and beats out his weary life.

For Philip's dwelling fronted on the street,
The latest house to landward; but behind,
With one small gate that open'd on the waste,
Flourish'd a little garden square and wall'd :       730
And in it throve an ancient evergreen,
A yewtree, and all round it ran a walk
Of shingle, and a walk divided it:

But Enoch shunn'd the middle walk and stole
Up by the wall, behind the yew; and thence     735
That which he better might have shunn'd, if griefs
Like his have worse or better, Enoch saw.

For cups and silver on the burnish'd board
Sparkled and shone; so genial was the hearth:
And on the right hand of the hearth he saw     740
Philip, the slighted suitor of old times,
Stout, rosy, with his babe across his knees;
And o'er her second father stoopt a girl,
A later but a loftier Annie Lee,
Fair-hair'd and tall, and from her lifted hand     745
Dangled a length of ribbon and a ring
To tempt the babe, who rear'd his creasy arms,
Caught at and ever miss'd it, and they laugh'd;
And on the left hand of the hearth he saw
The mother glancing often toward her babe,     750
But turning now and then to speak with him,
Her son, who stood beside her tall and strong,
And saying that which pleased him, for he smiled.

Now when the dead man come to life beheld
His wife his wife no more, and saw the babe     755
Hers, yet not his, upon the father's knee,
And all the warmth, the peace, the happiness,
And his own children tall and beautiful,
And him, that other, reigning in his place,
Lord of his rights and of his children's love, —     760
Then he, tho' Miriam Lane had told him all,
Because things seen are mightier than things heard,
Stagger'd and shook, holding the branch, and fear'd
To send abroad a shrill and terrible cry,

Which in one moment, like the blast of doom,          765
Would shatter all the happiness of the hearth.


    He therefore turning softly like a thief,
Lest the harsh shingle should grate underfoot,
And feeling all along the garden-wall,
Lest he should swoon and tumble and be found,          770
Crept to the gate, and open'd it, and closed,
As lightly as a sick man's chamber-door,
Behind him, and came out upon the waste.


    And there he would have knelt, but that his knees
Were feeble, so that falling prone he dug          775
His fingers into the wet earth, and pray'd.


    "Too hard to bear! why did they take me thence?
O God Almighty, blessed Saviour, Thou
That didst uphold me on my lonely isle,
Uphold me, Father, in my loneliness          780
A little longer! aid me, give me strength
Not to tell her, never to let her know.
Help me not to break in upon her peace.
My children too! must I not speak to these?
They know me not.   I should betray myself.          785
Never: No father's kiss for me — the girl
So like her mother, and the boy, my son."


    There speech and thought and nature fail'd a little,
And he lay tranced; but when he rose and paced
Back toward his solitary home again,          790
All down the long and narrow street he went
Beating in upon his weary brain,

As tho' it were the burthen of a song,
"Not to tell her, never to let her know."

   He was not all unhappy.  His resolve    795
Upbore him, and firm faith, and evermore
Prayer from a living source within the will,
And beating up thro' all the bitter world,
Like fountains of sweet water in the sea,
Kept him a living soul.  "This miller's wife,"    800
He said to Miriam, "that you spoke about,
Has she no fear that her first husband lives?"
"Ay, ay, poor soul," said Miriam, "fear enow!
If you could tell her you had seen him dead,
Why, that would be her comfort;" and he thought    805
"After the Lord has call'd me she shall know,
I wait his time," and Enoch set himself,
Scorning an alms, to work whereby to live.
Almost to all things could he turn his hand.
Cooper he was and carpenter, and wrought    810
To make the boatmen fishing-nets, or help'd
At lading and unlading the tall barks,
That brought the stinted commerce of those days;
Thus earn'd a scanty living for himself;
Yet since he did but labor for himself,    815
Work without hope, there was not life in it
Whereby the man could live; and as the year
Roll'd itself round again to meet the day
When Enoch had return'd, a languor came
Upon him, gentle sickness, gradually    820
Weakening the man, till he could do no more,
But kept the house, his chair, and last his bed.
And Enoch bore his weakness cheerfully.
For sure no gladlier does the stranded wreck

See thro' the gray skirts of a lifting squall          825
The boat that bears the hope of life approach
To save the life despair'd of, than he saw
Death dawning on him, and the close of all.

  For thro' that dawning gleam'd a kindlier hope
On Enoch thinking "after I am gone,          830
Then may she learn I lov'd her to the last."
He call'd aloud for Miriam Lane and said
"Woman, I have a secret — only swear,
Before I tell you — swear upon the book
Not to reveal it, till you see me dead."          835
"Dead," clamor'd the good woman, "hear him talk !
I warrant, man, that we shall bring you round."
"Swear," added Enoch sternly, " on the book."
And on the book, half-frighted, Miriam swore.
Then Enoch rolling his gray eyes upon her,          840
"Did you know Enoch Arden of this town ?"
"Know him ?" she said, "I knew him far away.
Ay, ay, I mind him coming down the street ;
Held his head high, and cared for no man, he."
Slowly and sadly Enoch answer'd her ;          845
"His head is low, and no man cares for him.
I think I have not three days more to live ;
I am the man."   At which the woman gave
A half-incredulous, half-hysterical cry.
"You Arden, you ! nay, — sure he was a foot          850
Higher than you be."   Enoch said again
" My God has bow'd me down to what I am ;
My grief and solitude have broken me ;
Nevertheless, know you that I am he
Who married — but that name has twice been changed —
I married her who married Philip Ray.          856

Sit, listen." Then he told her of his voyage,
His wreck, his lonely life, his coming back,
His gazing in on Annie, his resolve,
And how he kept it. As the woman heard,      860
Fast flow'd the current of her easy tears,
While in her heart she yearn'd incessantly
To rush abroad all round the little haven,
Proclaiming Enoch Arden and his woes;
But awed and promise-bounden she forbore,      865
Saying only, "See your bairns before you go!
Eh, let me fetch 'em, Arden," and arose
Eager to bring them down, for Enoch hung
A moment on her words, but then replied:

"Woman, disturb me not now at the last,      870
But let me hold my purpose till I die.
Sit down again; mark me and understand,
While I have power to speak. I charge you now,
When you shall see her, tell her that I died
Blessing her, praying for her, loving her;      875
Save for the bar between us, loving her
As when she laid her head beside my own.
And tell my daughter Annie, whom I saw
So like her mother, that my latest breath
Was spent in blessing her and praying for her.      880
And tell my son that I died blessing him.
And say to Philip that I blest him too;
He never meant us anything but good.
But if my children care to see me dead,
Who hardly knew me living, let them come,      885
I am their father; but she must not come,
For my dead face would vex her after-life.
And now there is but one of all my blood

Who will embrace me in the world-to-be:
This hair is his: she cut it off and gave it,          890
And I have borne it with me all these years,
And thought to bear it with me to my grave;
But now my mind is changed, for I shall see him,
My babe in bliss: wherefore when I am gone,
Take, give her this, for it may comfort her:          895
It will moreover be a token to her,
That I am he."

             He ceased; and Miriam Lane
Made such a voluble answer promising all,
That once again he roll'd his eyes upon her
Repeating all he wish'd, and once again          900
She promised.

            Then the third night after this,
While Enoch slumber'd motionless and pale,
And Miriam watch'd and dozed at intervals,
There came so loud a calling of the sea,
That all the houses in the haven rang.          905
He woke, he rose, he spread his arms abroad
Crying with a loud voice "A sail! a sail!
I am saved"; and so fell back and spoke no more.

So passed the strong heroic soul away.
And when they buried him the little port          910
Had seldom seen a costlier funeral.

# NOTES.

## THE RIME OF THE ANCIENT MARINER.

*The Ancient Mariner* was first published in *Lyrical Ballads* in 1798. Its title was *The Rime of the Ancyent Marinere in Seven Parts.* In the second edition of *Lyrical Ballads* (1800) this was changed to *The Ancient Mariner, a Poet's Reverie.* The text was much changed from the original, and the extremely archaic spelling was modernized. The texts of 1802 and 1805 were essentially the same as that of 1800. In 1817 the ballad was reprinted in *Sibylline Leaves,* with a Latin motto, some textual changes, the marginal gloss added, and the grotesquely horrible element made less prominent. An argument prefixed to the edition of 1798 was omitted in the succeeding editions until that of 1817, when it was restored.

The occasion of *Lyrical Ballads* has been related by both Coleridge and Wordsworth, each giving some details omitted by the other. Wordsworth tells us that the book grew out of a plan intended to furnish them with money for defraying the expenses of a walking excursion among the Quantock Hills. The sum needed was £5, but the work soon more than sufficed to raise that amount, and the slender anonymous volume did more than any other book to restore the romantic element to English verse.

In *Biographia Literaria* Coleridge has recorded the poetic principles on which the *Lyrical Ballads* is based. In conversations with Wordsworth they frequently discussed "the two cardinal points of poetry, the power of exciting the sympathy of the reader by a faithful adherence to the truth of nature, and the power of giving the interest of novelty by the modifying colours of the imagination." [1] It was decided to compose a series of poems of two sorts. "In one the incidents and agents were to be, in part at least, supernatural; and the excellence aimed at was to consist in the interesting of the affections

[1] *Biographia Literaria,* Chapter **XIV.**

by the dramatic truth of such emotions, as would naturally accompany such situations, supposing them real. For the second class, subjects were to be chosen from ordinary life ; the characters and incidents were to be such as will be found in every village and its vicinity where there is a meditative and feeling mind to seek after them or to notice them when they present themselves." [1]

Thus originated the plan of *Lyrical Ballads.* Coleridge undertook the supernatural and romantic parts, while Wordsworth contributed the incidents from common life. *The Ancient Mariner* was the only poem that Coleridge furnished, though he began *Christabel* and *The Dark Ladie,* " in which," he says, " I should have more nearly realized my ideal than I had done in my first attempt."

The source of the plot has been the subject of numerous conjectures. According to Coleridge, the story was founded on a dream of a Stowey friend named Cruikshank. In Shelvock's *Voyages* occurs a passage describing the albatrosses observed as the ship was doubling Cape Horn. Wordsworth suggested that the " old navigator " be represented as having killed one of the birds, and that the tutelary spirit of that region seek vengeance upon him for the crime. In an article, *The Source of the Ancient Mariner* (*Athenæum*, 1890), Mr. Ivor James maintains that the source of the story is Captain Thomas James's *Strange and Dangerous Voyage*, published at London, 1633. Still another theory is that the poet gained his idea from a letter written to Macarius by Paulinus, Bishop of Nola, in the latter part of the fourth century. The letter relates " the astounding wonders concerning the shipwreck of an old man." In this tale, the old man is the sole survivor from the crews of a numerous fleet, a " Crew of Angels " navigated the ship, and the " Pilot of the World " steered the vessel to the Lucanian Shore."

Whatever the occasion or the source of the ballad may have been, the fact remains that *The Ancient Mariner* is in all points one of the most wonderful creations in all literature. A few lines from Lowell will suffice to show the general attitude of criticism. " It is enough for us here that he (Coleridge) has written some of the most poetical poetry in the language, and one poem, *The Ancient Mariner*, not only unparalleled, but unapproached in its kind, and that kind of the rarest. . . . Coleridge has taken the old ballad measure and given

---

[1] *Biographia Literaria*, Chapter XIV.

to it, by indefinable charm wholly his own, all the sweetness, all the melody and compass, of a symphony. And how picturesque it is in the proper sense of the word. I know nothing like it. There is not a description in it. It is all picture. Descriptive poets generally confuse us with multiplicity of detail; we cannot see their forest for trees; but Coleridge never errs in this way. With instinctive tact he touches the right chord of association, and is satisfied as we also are. I should find it hard to explain the singular charm of his diction, there is so much nicety of art and purpose in it, whether for music or for meaning. . . . The words seem common words enough, but in the order of them, in the choice, variety, and position of the vowel sounds, they become magical. The most decrepit vocable in the language throws away its crutches to dance and sing at his piping. . . . More bits of Coleridge have imbedded themselves in my memory than of any other poet who delighted my youth, unless I should except the sonnets of Shakespeare. This argues perfectness of expression." [1]

1. Compare this ballad with others of the sea : Tennyson's *Revenge ;* Longfellow's *Wreck of the Hesperus ; Sir Patrick Spens ;* and *The Ship of the Fiend.* Note the similarity of the introductory stanzas. The opening verse is characteristic of the ballad. Cf. *Proud Lady Margaret, Five Flowers i' the Valley, The Twa Sisters O' Binnornie,* etc.

Why was a wedding guest selected to hear the mariner's tale ? Why not a churchyard sexton ?

2. **One of three.** Why not one of four or five ? Notice throughout the poem that the prevailing numbers are three, five, seven, and nine. The odd numbers have always been regarded as proper to the mystical and supernatural, — nine muses, seven wonders of the world, three fates, etc.

11. Cf. *Macbeth,* Act V. Sc. 3, l. 2.

14. Walter Pater (*Appreciations,* p. 101) remarks that the unity of this poem is secured in part by the skill with which the incidents of the wedding feast are made to break in dreamily from time to time upon the main story. The vividness of the narrative is greatly increased by having the mariner relate his own experiences.

15-16. Wordsworth furnished these lines.

[1] *Democracy and Other Addresses,* pp. 98, 99.

23. There are many dialectic and archaic forms in this poem. Why?

25 ff. The effect of the monosyllables should be noted here. Cf. Shakespeare's *Sonnets;* also Tennyson's lyric, *Ask Me No More*, and *Voyage;* Longfellow's *Discoverer of the North Cape.*

34. This simile occurs frequently in the old ballads. Read Burns's lyric, *A Red, Red Rose.* De Koven has furnished a beautiful setting for the song.

35. There is a similar line in *The Ballad of the Dark Ladie.*

36. **Minstrelsy** means a band of musicians. They catered to the amusement of the nobles, and in ancient halls there was usually a gallery reserved for their use.

37. What does the uneasiness of the wedding guest show concerning the progress of the tale? When does the interest of the story banish all thought of the festivities? It has been objected by some critics that Coleridge shows an undignified haste to transport us to "the æsthetically necessary region," i.e. the realm of the supernatural. What is your opinion? Read W. Watson, *Excursions in Criticism*, p. 98.

55. **Clifts.** Usually written cliffs. Robinson Crusoe "climbed up the clifts of the shore."

63. The incident of the Albatross was suggested by Wordsworth.

79 ff. The bond of fellowship between man and beast is broken, the crime is committed, and vengeance must follow. Read the *Wanderings of Cain* and note a passage similar in spirit. Cf. also *Macbeth, Richard III.*, Stevenson's *Markheim* and *Master of Ballantrae*, Hawthorne's *House of the Seven Gables*, and the opening chapter of Aldrich's *Stillwater Tragedy.* Coleridge's short poem, *The Raven*, has the same moral as *The Ancient Mariner*, — the Greek idea of Nemesis. The spirit of reverence for life, whether of man or beast, often appears in our literature.

93. Why did the mariner shoot the Albatross? The student should note carefully the changing opinions of the sailors. Why did they condemn the mariner's action?

104. In *Sibylline Leaves* (1817) this line reads, —

"The furrow streamed off free."

The following note was added by Coleridge: "I had not been long on board a ship before I perceived that this was the image as seen by a spectator from the shore, or from another vessel. From the ship itself the wake appears like a brook flowing off from the stern." The earlier reading reappeared in subsequent editions. It is certainly more euphonius, and Coleridge was evidently willing to allow the unimportant inaccuracy in order to gain a greater beauty of expression.

106. **Silent sea**. Cf. *Kubla Khan*, ll. 1-5, and Poe's *Annabel Lee*.

117-118. Cf. *Hamlet*, Act II. Sc. 2, ll. 460 ff., and *Macbeth*, Act V. Sc. 8, ll. 22 ff.

123. **O Christ**. Cf. this suggestion of a belief in a higher power with the thought of Part V., "slid into my soul." Note its value in the development of character of one who seemed devoid of even a conscience. What is its force psychologically in the poem ?

127. There are passages similar to this in both Shakespeare and Middleton. Cf. the witch scenes in *Macbeth* and scattered passages in *The Witch*.

128. Cf. *Ode to the Departing Year*, Stanza III. l. 21.

141-142. The punishment of course is by retributive justice, sufficiently severe to have been ordained by Fate. Cf. *Hamlet* and Æschylus's *Libation Pourers*. How far in the progress of the narrative does Part II. take us ?

143. What is the rhetorical function of this stanza ?

164. The word **grin** is here used with peculiar suggestiveness. One can almost see the distorted face, with muscles drawn from the agony of thirst. In *Table Talk* (May 31, 1830) Coleridge writes: " I took the thought of *grinning for joy* from my companion's remark to me when we had climbed to the top of Plinlimmon, and were fairly dead with thirst. We could not speak from the constriction till we found a little puddle under a stone. He said to me, ' You grinned like an idiot ! ' He had done the same." Cf. Milton, *Paradise Lost*, Bk. II. ll. 845 ff.

169. With this description of the phantom ship, cf. Longfellow's *Phantom Ship* and *Ballad of Carmilhan*. Also Whittier's *Dead Ship of Harpswell*.

178. **Heaven's Mother**. Here, as in several other places, is suggested the religion prevailing at the time in which the story is placed. Can you determine in any way when that time was ?

185 ff. In the first edition (*Lyrical Ballads*) the following stanza was inserted : —

> "*His* bones were black with many a crack,
>   All black and bare, I ween ;
>   Jet-black and bare, save where with rust
>   Of mouldy damps and charnel crust
>   They're patch'd with purple and green."

The last two verses of the next stanza read, —

> "And she is far liker Death than he ;
>   Her flesh makes the still air cold."

Can you give any reason for the change ?  Coleridge, commenting on Milton's description of Death (*Paradise Lost*, Bk. II. ll. 666 ff.), remarks : "The grandest efforts of poetry are when the imagination is called forth to produce, not a distinct form, but a strong working of the mind, still offering what is still repelled, and again creating what is again rejected ; the result being what the poet wishes to impress, viz. the substitution of a sublime feeling of unimaginable for mere images."  Cf. Job iv. 13–17 and Rev. vi. 2, 8.

197.  Cf. *Macbeth*, Act I. Sc. 3, beginning, —

> "The weird sisters, hand in hand,
>   Posters of the sea and land." . . .

223.  Compare this verse with the closing lines of each other part. Note that each ends with an allusion to the Albatross.  Why ?

226–227.  These lines are Wordsworth's.

232 ff.  In these lines the poet has illustrated his principle quoted above (note to ll. 185 ff.).  The horror and terror of the description is comparable with that of Lady Macbeth (Act V. Sc. 1) or that of Hamlet's uncle (Act III. Sc. 3).

238.  Cf. Milton's *Paradise Lost*, Bk. VI. l. 767, and Spenser's *Faerie Queen*, Bk. II. Canto XII. l. 25 ; Rev. xiv. 1.

292.  Cf. Shelley's *Queen Mab*, opening stanza, Wordsworth's *To Sleep*, Coleridge's *The Pains of Sleep*, Keats's *Endymion*, Bk. I. ll. 453 ff., Sidney's *Sonnet to Sleep*, *Macbeth*, Act II. Sc. 2, l. 7, and *II. King Henry*, Act IV. Sc. 1, l. 531.

295.  Cf. Browning's *Christmas Eve*, Stanza XX., for a very striking similarity in phraseology.

297.  **Silly** means useless (because of the drought).

358.  Cf. this grouping of details to emphasize the feeling of peace and blessedness with ll. 232 ff., where the accumulated incidents por-

tray increasing horror; also with ll. 119 ff., where a similar effect is produced.

359. Cf. poems by Wordsworth, Shelley, and Hogg to *The Skylark.* Read also Coleridge's *Fears in Solitude.* From Chaucer down, skylarks and nightingales have been beloved by all poets.

387-388 ff. This stanza suggests Edgar Allan Poe, whose favorite device was the echo effect. See *The Raven, Ulalume, Lenore, Annabel Lee,* etc.

402. What is the rhetorical purpose of this stanza?

408. In your opinion, has the mariner been sufficiently punished?

414. Coleridge uses the same expression in his drama *Osorio,* —

> "O woman,
> I have stood silent as a slave before thee."

420. Cf. Wordsworth's *Intimations of Immortality,* Stanza II.

446. Most of us have experienced this same feeling when walking in lonely places. The description takes us back to primitive conditions, when superstition was a prominent part of religion. The editor remembers very distinctly his own fears when a boy, — a certain dark road through an unfrequented wood filled him with vague, nameless terror. Read *Christabel* for a description of similar feelings on land. Cf. Spenser's *Faerie Queen,* Bk. II. Canto VII. St. 26 and 27. Also Lamb's *Essays* (*Witches and Other Night Fears*), where this stanza is quoted and comment made on Coleridge's imaginative power.

472. "How pleasantly, how reassuringly the whole nightmare story is made to end among the clear, fresh sounds and lights of the bay where it began." — WALTER PATER.

Cf. Longfellow's *The Bridge.*

473. Cf. *Remorse,* Act III. Sc. 1 (song).

490 ff. Wordsworth suggested this incident.

514 ff. Cf. Goldsmith's *The Hermit,* also *Christabel,* Part II. (lines describing the sacristan).

578 ff. Cf. *Remorse,* Act I. Sc. 1, ll. 20-25, speech of Zulinez, Don Alvar's faithful attendant. Also Wordsworth's *Intimations of Immortality,* ll. 19-23.

601 *ad finem.* With this conclusion the spirit of universal love as it has appeared in literature should be considered. A few poems that

best illustrate this feeling are here mentioned. The student should find others for himself. Coleridge, *To a Young Ass* and *Religious Musings;* Wordsworth, *Hart-leap Well;* Burns, *To a Mouse, On Seeing a Wounded Hare Leap by Me, Death of Poor Mailie, A Winter Night,* etc.; Cowper, *Epitaph on a Hare* (*Task*, Bk. III.). In *Table Talk* Coleridge cites and answers two objections often made against *The Ancient Mariner:* "Mrs. Barbauld once told me that she admired *The Ancient Mariner* very much, but that there were two faults in it, — it was improbable and had no moral. As to the probability, I owned that that might admit some question, but as to the want of moral, I told her that in my judgment the poem had too much; and that the only or chief fault, if I might say so, was the obtrusion of the moral sentiment so openly on the reader, as a principle or cause of action in a work of such pure imagination. It ought to have had no more moral than the Arabian Nights Tale."

## SOHRAB AND RUSTUM.

Arnold's poem is based on an episode in the *Shāh Nāmeh* or *Book of Kings*, the great Persian epic written by Firdusi in the tenth century A.D. In the main he has closely followed the original, but in minor details he has adapted the "tale of tears," as the incident is described, to the needs of his own poem. The *Shah Nameh* is to Persian what the *Cid* is to Spanish, the *Iliad* and *Odyssey* to Greek, the *Æneid* to Latin, *Paradise Lost* to English.

Rūstum, son of Zal, is the great hero of the epic. During one of his many excursions he married a beautiful maiden, Tamīneh, but a fresh adventure soon called him from her. Sōhrab was their son. The mother, fearing her boy would be taken from her, sent word to Rustum that the child was a girl, and in *her* (worthless encumbrance!) the father had no further interest. As the boy grew up he came to know that the mighty Rustum was his father, and no persuasion availed to keep him from seeking him far and wide. The poem opens on the occasion of an invasion of Persia by the Tartars — among them Sohrab, not the leader, but their bravest champion. To illustrate Arnold's skill in rounding out and completing the story, attention will be directed here and there through the poem, to points in which he has modified the original.

**1. And.** The word shows the episodic nature of the poem. This use, in the sense of "to continue the narrative," is frequent in the Bible. Cf. Exodus ix. 21, xxxi. 1, etc.

**2. The Oxus** is now called the Amoo Darya. Milton mentions the Oxus, *Paradise Lost*, Bk. XI. l. 389. Cf. these opening lines with those which conclude the poem, ll. 875 *ad finem.*

**3.** Tartar is the general name for the many nomadic tribes that inhabit Central Asia and Southern Russia. The Kalmuck tribe, celebrated by De Quincey in *The Flight of a Tartar Tribe*, is one of them.

**9.** Cf. with this description the restless wandering of King Henry V in his camp at Agincourt. It is found in the chorus prefixed to Act IV. of *King Henry V.*

**11.** *Pērän-Wīsä* was a Turanian chief and the military leader of King Afrasiab's forces. Iran, the Persian empire, was separated from Turania by the river Oxus.

**12.** The relative luxury of the Persians compared with the hardy Tartars is suggested in l. 192.

**15. Pamere** is a plateau 16,000 feet high, north of Afghanistan. The natives call it the "Roof of the World."

**19.** In summer the river was flooded.

**29.** Cf. *Romeo and Juliet*, Act II. Sc. 3, ll. 35 ff.

**38. Afrasiab** was king of the Turanians and numbered among his forces many Tartar tribes (*vid.* ll. 119–134). He was said to be as strong as a lion and his shadow extended for miles. He was a direct descendant of Tur, one of Feridoon's three sons. The *Shah Nameh* is taken up largely with accounts of the many Turanian invasions. At the time of this episode Afrasiab's power was weakening. The house of Zal (Rustum's father) had pledged itself to the expulsion of the invaders, a promise fulfilled through the prowess of Rustum, who defeated Afrasiab and compelled his retreat across the Oxus.

**40. Samarcand** is a city in what is now Russian Turkestan. It is to-day a centre of Mohammedan culture and learning.

**42. Ader-baijan** (Äzer-bīyan), a northwestern province of Persia, on the Turanian frontier.

**49.** Here is the motive that furnishes the tragic element of the story. Classical students will do well to look up the interview between Telemachus and Menelaus, *Odyssey*, Bk. IV.

H

56. Cf. the challenge sent by Paris to Menelaus, *Iliad*, Bk. **III.** Also the conversation between David and Saul, 1 Sam. xvii. 36 ff.

59–60. The aphorisms in these lines illustrate what was said in the biographical sketch concerning Arnold's care of details while never losing sight of the whole.

63. Is this an Oriental way of expressing sympathy or affection ?

78. Cf. ll. 221 ff.

82. **Seistan** is a province of Afghanistan. There is also a lake of the same name. **Zal** was Rustum's father. He was descended from Benjamin, son of Jacob. At birth his hair was snow-white, and for this Saum, his father, left the child to die in the mountains. He was, however, found and cared for by a wonderful creature, part human and part bird, called the Simurgh, that carried him away to its nest. Here he was safely kept until his penitent father prayed that he might be restored to him. In his youth Zal ruled with the wisdom that belongs to silvered hair.

85. Cf. l. 226.

86 ff. Peran-Wisa's solicitude for Rustum's son is an invention of Arnold's. Firdusi does not mention it. Why does Arnold introduce it ?

94 ff. In *Blackwood's Magazine*, Vol. LXXV., is a severe criticism on this analysis of Peran-Wisa's toilet. There is in this minuteness a characteristic of Arnold's style, but the effect here is well-nigh ludicrous and furnishes one of the few instances in the poem where he becomes prosaic. Another is 265 and the following lines. A man at his toilet is not a highly poetic theme.

99. The **staff** was a primitive sign of leadership. Cf. *Iliad*, Bk. I. ll. 15 ff., 234 ff., and 225. See also Genesis xxxii. 10 ; 2 Kings iv. 29.

110 ff. The general effect of this geographical passage is a gain in variety. Many poets have delighted in long catalogues of men or places. Cf. *Iliad*, Bk. II. ll. 484 ff., Chaucer's *Prologue*, ll. 429 ff., and Milton's *Paradise Lost*, Bk. XI. ll. 379 ff. Most of the places here mentioned may be found on any modern map of Afghanistan, Persia, and Turkestan. **Khiva** and **Bokhara** are cities in Turkestan. The **Attruck** empties into the Caspian, the **Jaxartes** into the Aral Sea. The **Tukas** were soldiers from the various provinces. **Ferghana** is a province of Turkestan. **Kipchak** is a town on the Oxus in independent Tartary. **Kirghizzies** are a tribe of Central Asia. The

**Kalmucks** dwelt in upper Asia, and **Khorassan** was a province of Eastern Persia.

150 ff. Cf. Goliath's challenge, 1 Sam. xvii. 4 ff.

160. **Cabool** is the capital of Afghanistan.

161. The more common name for the **Indian Caucasus** is the Hindoo Koosh Mountains.

177. The use of epithets is a characteristic of the epics. Cf. those applied to Achilles, "swift-footed," "fiery-hearted," etc., *Iliad*, Bk. I. ll. 84, 121, 148, etc. Agamemnon in one of his angry tirades against Achilles describes him as having the "heart of a stag." See *Iliad*, Bk. I. l. 225.

178. **Aloof he sits.** With this, cf. Achilles nursing his wrath at the loss of his prize Briseïs, *Iliad*, Bk. I. ll. 348 ff.

192. Cf. l. 12 and note.

195. Cf. with this embassy that of Ulysses and his companions to Achilles. In the latter instance the proffers of hospitality were accepted. *Iliad*, Bk. IX. ll. 240 ff. (Bryant's Translation).

208–209. Cf. with this the Preacher's analysis of times and their purposes. Ecclesiastes iii. 1 ff.

214. The *Shah Nameh* recounts at some length the artifices employed by Tamineh to deceive Rustum. She went so far as to send with Sohrab an attendant whose business it was to avert a meeting between father and son. The student will recognize in this sentence the reason for all the evil that followed.

215. In the *Shah Nameh* occurs the following passage. Rustum has seen the youthful champion, and thus describes him to the Persian monarch, —

> "Circled by chiefs this glorious youth was seen,
> Of lofty stature and majestic mien;
> No Tartar region gave that hero birth:
> Some happier portion of the spacious earth;
> Tall as the graceful cypress he appears;
> Like Sām, the brave, his warrior-front he rears!"

> (Trans. by JAMES ATKINSON.)

217. **Iran's chiefs**, i.e. Persian chiefs. The Persians called their country Iran. Tradition says that the Persians and Turks were descended from two brothers, — Iran and Turan, respectively.

221. **Go to.** A Hebraism frequently used in the Bible. Gen. xi. 3 ; Isa. v. 5, etc.

222. **Kai Khosroo** has been identified with Cyrus the Great, who lived about 550 B.C. In placing the story of Sohrab and Rustum in his reign, Arnold has varied the statement of the *Shah Nameh*, which puts the incident during the reign of the "weak and brainless monarch," Kai Kaoos. Can you assign any reason for this ?

233. Modern Afghanistan includes ancient Seistan, where Zal lived.

265. With this description of the arming of Rustum, cf. that of Achilles, *Iliad*, Bk. XIX. ll. 440 ff. Arnold's description here, as in the instance of Peran-Wisa, is prosaic in the extreme. He succeeds much better with the horse Ruksh, ll. 275 ff.

270. In legendary lore the horse of the hero is an important character. Achilles's horse Xanthus, Aquiline, the horse in *Jerusalem Delivered*, Babieca, of the *Cid*, are as interesting as their masters. Rustum, when a youth, long sought a horse for his knightly use. He tried many in vain, and at last, roaming among the flocks at Cabul, found a wonderful steed of marvellous strength, rose colored, who had permitted no man to mount him until his preordained master, Rustum, appeared. It had been predicted that Rustum, mounted upon Ruksh, would save the world.

286. The island of **Bahrein** is famous for its pearl-fishing.

288. **Tale.** Cf. Milton's *L'Allegro*, l. 67. Also Exodus v. 8.

315. **In a queen's garden,** etc. "Beautiful arbors or gardens are frequently built within the walls of Eastern palaces. They are fancifully fitted up, and supplied with reservoirs, fountains, and flower trees. These romantic garden pavilions are called *kiosks* in Turkey, and are generally situated upon an eminence near a running stream." — ATKINSON.

322 ff. In this conversation between Sohrab and Rustum, Arnold has followed the *Shah Nameh* more closely than in any other part of the narrative.

331. Cf. ll. 229, 447, 709.

340. The picture is strikingly Homeric. Cf. *Iliad*, Bk. I. ll. 500 ff., where Thetis makes her prayer to Zeus to avenge the affront to Achilles.

343.     " Art thou not Rustum, whose exploits sublime
        Endear his name thro' every distant clime ? "

In answer to this, Rustum denies his name, —

> " I boast no station of exalted birth,
> No proud pretensions to distinguished worth ;
> To him inferior, no such powers are mine,
> No offspring I of Nirum's glorious line."

> — *Shah Nameh* (Trans. by ATKINSON).

**347.** In his numerous adventures, Rustum owed his success to his craftiness as much as to his strength. " Crafty " is one of Homer's stock epithets for Ulysses.

**381.** Cf. the sneers of Cassius at Cæsar. *Julius Cæsar*, Act I. Sc. 2, ll. 120 ff. Also *Macbeth*, Act III. Sc. 4, l. 106.

**397.** The people of Persia are all Fatalists, a fact that explains Sohrab's secrecy, —

> . . . " he explored the crowded field,
> Nor once the secret of his birth revealed ;
> Heaven will'd it so."

> — *Shah Nameh* (Trans. by ATKINSON).

**409.** The club is the more natural weapon of primitive conflicts. Cf. the stories of Hercules. Also *Odyssey*, Bk. IX. l. 322 ; *Æneid*, Bk. III. l. 659 ; and *Paradise Lost*, Bk. I. ll. 292–295.

**412.** The **Hyphasis** and **Hydaspes** are rivers in Northern India. The modern names are Jhelum (Zhitum) and Beas.

**420 ff.** Cf. David's clemency to Saul in the cave of the wilderness of Engedi. I Sam. xxiv.

**428.** The faulty order here reminds one of the " women who were seen digging a well with straw hats."

**434.** The idea of wading in blood is frequently met in literature. Cf. *Macbeth*, Act III. Sc. 4, l. 136 ; *Midsummer Night's Dream*, Act III. Sc. 2, l. 47 ; and Dryden's *Œdipus*, Act IV. Sc. 1.

**481.** Classic writers often veiled their warriors in cloud. Cf. *Æneid*, Bk. I. ll. 497 ff., and Bk. IX. ll. 33 ff. ; *Iliad*, Bk. III. ll. 465 ff. Also Spenser, *Faerie Queen*, Bk. I. Canto V. Stanza 13. In the *Shah Nameh*, the conflict is not confined to one day ; Sohrab and Rustum contend three times. The first day's battle is ended by the approach of night, as was the single combat between Hector and Ajax, *Iliad*, Bk. VII. ll. 282 ff. In order to increase the rapidity of the action and deepen its dignity, Arnold has compressed the three battles into a single conflict. Suggest other motives he may have had for thus modifying the original.

501 ff.   The sympathy of animals for their masters, according to the ancient writers, often found utterance in human speech.   Cf. Numbers xxii.   Also *Iliad*, Bk. XIX. ll. 393 ff.

527.   Cf. Sohrab's words of triumph, ll. 427 ff.

590.   **My mother**, etc.   Sohrab's mother was Tamineh, a Tartar princess.   The *Shah Nameh* tells us that she was enamoured of Rustum from hearing of his knightly deeds.   On one occasion her emissaries stole Ruksh and led him away to Ader-baijam while Rustum was asleep.   When he awoke, the hero tracked his horse to Samenegan, capital of Turan.   He was met by the king, anxious to honor so distinguished a visitor.   Rustum refused the proffered hospitality and demanded his horse.   The king promised to return Ruksh, and while search was being made Rustum accepted the royal hospitality.   Meantime Tamineh's maidens arranged for a meeting between their mistress and Rustum.   Eventually they were married, but shortly after the nuptials Rustum, as has been already related, was summoned by the king to lead important campaigns.   It is worthy of note in this connection that in the Orient a strong attachment to the mother is universal.

625.   . . . **her father**, etc.   That is, the king of Samenegan.

626.   The wandering guest was Rustum.   Cf. note on l. 590.

658 ff.   Here Arnold has again modified the story of the *Shah Nameh*, which says that Rustum gave Tamineh an onyx stone as an amulet, which should be given to their child as a means of identification.   For this is substituted the seal pricked into Sohrab's arm.   Why?   The onyx united the wearer to deeds of valor such as those performed by Neriman, Sohrab's famous ancestor.

679.   The marvellous Simurgh that cared for Zal when his father left him to die on the mountains.   See introductory note to this poem.

738–740.   Cf. last two lines of Bk. XX., *Iliad*.

751.   The **Helmund** is a river of Afghanistan.

763.   The **Moorghab, Tejend**, and **Kohik** are rivers of Turkestan that are lost in the great desert south of Bokhara.   The **northern Sir** is the Jaxartes or Syr Daria.

783 ff.   The *Shah Nameh* gives an extended account of the funeral rites in honor of Sohrab.   A thousand horses were sacrificed; then a

procession led by the great chief bore Sohrab's body to Seistan. Zal shed "tears of blood," Rudabeh loudly bewailed the stripling's doom, and thousands, with rent garments and loosely flowing hair, filled the air with shrieks and clamors. The rites concluded, the corpse was covered with a yellow robe and closed in a bier of aloes. Above his body was raised a sepulchral mound, "formed like a charger's hoof." The last sixty lines of the episode are devoted to a description of Tamineh's grief for her lost son, —

> "Day after day she thus indulged her grief,
> Night after night, disdaining all relief ;
> At length worn out — from earthly anguish riven,
> The mother's spirit joined her child in Heaven."
>
> (Trans. by ATKINSON.)

830. Kai Khosroo after Afrasiab's death determined to spend the rest of his days in retirement. He therefore divided his kingdom among his nobles, and with a few attendants went to a spring fixed upon as the place of his rest. Then he suddenly disappeared, and all who went with him were drowned on the return voyage. From the words of Sohrab in these lines we should infer that Rustum was among those who perished. But according to the *Shah Nameh* the great champion was killed through the wiles of his brother Shugdad when they were on a hunting expedition.

861. **Jemshid** was a mythical Persian king, whose glory and misfortune are a constant theme of admiration among the poets of Persia.

878. Chorasmia is the ancient name of Karissim, or Kharas, on the Oxus.

880. **Orgunjè** is a small village on the Oxus, about seventy miles below Khiva.

The closing lines of the poem illustrate a common characteristic of Mr. Arnold's verses. Peace after pain, rest after the turbulent passion of tragedy, is always realized. Read *Balder Dead*, *Tristram and Iseult*, *The Strayed Reveller*, etc. Wherever possible the student is advised to read the episode of *Sohrab and Rustum*, as translated by Atkinson. In Miss Rabb's *National Epics* the story of the *Shah Nameh* is told in a most entertaining manner. Interesting also are Chapters X. and XI. of Mrs. E. A. Reed's *Persian Literature*. In Charles Dudley Warner's *Library of the World's Best Literature* is a sketch of Firdusi, the author of the *Shah Nameh*.

## ENOCH ARDEN.

*Enoch Arden* was first published in 1864 in a volume entitled *Enoch Arden and Other Poems*. It is a narrative of humble life, like some of the tales by Wordsworth and Crabbe. The subject was not new. The adventures of a shipwrecked mariner have furnished themes for many writers of prose and of verse. Defoe's *Robinson Crusoe*, Lady Barnard's *Auld Robin Gray*, Crabbe's *Parting Hour*, Chamisso's *Salas y Gomez*, all treat the same subject. In 1858 Adelaide Procter published *Homeward Bound*, and to this poem Tennyson's idyll bears a strong resemblance. The story of Don Alvaro in *Gil Blas* also has marked similarities with *Enoch Arden*. *The Predecessors of Enoch Arden* is a subject very fully discussed by C. S. Brown in *Modern Language Notes* for June, 1897.

The poem is well suited to Tennyson's genius. The "short and simple annals of the poor" require no tragic passion in their narration. It has of course met adverse criticism. It has been said that the story is too simple for its elaborate setting, that it is loaded down with detail. Certain it is, however, that the narrative has had a wide popularity since its first publication, and that few of Tennyson's poems have been so generally read.

1. The nine opening lines serve the unity of the poem to an extent seldom found. "Out of the chord thus struck every future change will flow, and no unmeaning note is found within it." — *Quarterly Review*.

7. **Barrows** are sepulchral mounds, very common in England. Some are supposed to be older than the Roman conquest. The "mounds" of the United States are very similar.

32. Rolfe notes this line as "a good example of Tennyson's felicitous condensation of phrase."

36. With this line the supernatural element enters the poem. This is the first unconscious prophecy. The prophecies, Annie's dream, and her determination reached by the direction of a chance passage in the Bible, make the poem seem more natural and add a simple dignity to the humble hero's fate.

54. A **full sailor** is what we call "an able seaman."

58. This is one of the many "run-on" lines in the poem. Cf. l. 47. This repetition is Homeric. For the same effect, cf. ll. 46 and 86;

106, 120, and 128 ; 138, 169, and 171 ; 167 and 294 ; 67 an 270, and many others. The poem *Dora* furnishes other examples.

71–72.   Webb compares Coleridge's poem *Love*, 1.

80–81.   The melody of these lines helps to picture the joyfulness presented by the words.   What change in the verses accomplishes this end ?   Cf. ll. 507–509.

100.   Friday is a fast day in the Roman Catholic and English High Church.

112.   Enoch is represented throughout the poem wholly consistent with the description of him in this line.   Cf. ll. 127, 188, 208, etc.

123.   What quality does the direct question used here and in other places impart to the style ?

131.   This line has been variously explained by several editors.   It seems to mean simply that the cloud resembles an island flashed with light.

174–175.   Note in these lines the slight touch of the supernatural, which adds so much to the naturalness of the poem.   With Annie's presentiment on this occasion, compare the one after her second marriage, ll. 510–516.

193.   In this line is the second unconscious prophecy.   Cf. ll. 32, 212, 213 ; also note ll. 174–175.

212.   Cf. Acts xx. 38.   In this and the line following occur the third and fourth unconscious prophecies.

222 ff.   Enoch's parting words are simple and manly.   The deepest feeling is ever expressed in the fewest words, — more is felt than can be said.   For his Biblical quotations, see 1 Peter v. 7 ; Hebrews vi. 19 ; Psalms cxxxix. 7 and 9–10 ; and xcv. 5.   His words emphasize the truthful simplicity of his religion.

243.   The combination of literal and figurative statement is more frequently employed for humorous effect.   C. S. Brown cites a line from Tennyson's *Sea Dreams*, —

> " With all his conscience and one eye askew."

Also from Butler's *Hudibras*, III. 1, —

> " So Spanish heroes with their lances
> At once wound bulls and ladies' fancies."

370.   Cf. ll. 67 and 78.
383.   Cf. l. 75.

491. The method of divination here used by Annie is that known as Sortes Biblicæ or bibliomancy. The Bible is opened at random, and the first passage that is touched by the finger or that catches the eye is supposed to contain the desired direction. Before the introduction of Christianity the poets, particularly Homer and Virgil, were used in the same way. Bibliomancy was much used by the Puritans, and the custom may still be found among the lower classes of England and Scotland.

494. *Vid.* Judges iv. 5.

502. *Vid.* John xii. 13 ; Matthew xxi. 9 ; Mark xi. 10.

506. The use of the word **so** is peculiar. Used with the future or subjunctive it means *provided that.* It seems to include the idea " in this way," " on these terms." *Vid.* Abbott's *Shakespearian Grammar*, sec. 133.

507–509. Tennyson's superior art is illustrated in the scansion of these lines. The varying feeling represented in 508 and 509 are deftly suggested in the changed accent of merrily.

510–516. With this mysterious instinct, compare the presentiment in lines 174–175 and 609–612.

523–533, 537–549. These passages show Tennyson's power as a poet of the sea. Other illustrations may be read in *The Revenge, The Voyage, Sea Dreams*, etc.

561. **Death-in-life.** Cf. Coleridge's description of the woman Life-in-Death, *Ancient Mariner*, ll. 190 ff.

590 ff. Cf. *Ancient Mariner*, ll. 25 ff.

601. The **line,** of course, is the equator. Cf. Goldsmith's *Traveller*, l. 69.

609–613. The mysterious sympathy by which Enoch heard the far-distant pealing of the bells for Annie's marriage is another preternatural element in the story. For a description of a telepathic communication somewhat similar, read *Aylmer's Field*, ll. 578 ff. Classes interested in Tennyson's use of the supernatural will find further illustrations in *The Lover's Tale, Rizpah*, and *The Wreck.*

629. Read the opening lines of Coleridge's *Kubla Khan.*

640–641. Cf. Mark vii. 35 and Luke i. 64.

677. What was Tennyson's purpose in suggesting this change in the appearance of nature ? Compare with these lines the contrasting pictures in ll. 754 ff.

762. The thought is old, — Herodotus, Horace, Seneca, and many

*o*thers of more recent times have expressed it; but no one has furnished it with a setting that so powerfully forces the truth upon us as is done by Tennyson in this scene.

766. Enoch here wins his second great victory over self. What was his first?

782. "A low-toned or morbid artist would have made them meet, — the situation has been produced more than once in recent novels to the entire offence of all readers of refinement and sensibility." — TAINSH.

Is this your opinion?

803. **Enow** is an old plural form of "enough." The form is archaic and provincial. What character of this story frequently uses colloquial forms? Can you see any reason for this?

816–817. Read Coleridge's poem *Work without Hope* and Whittier's *Among the Hills*, 46 ff.

871–888. Blackwood comments on these lines as follows: "The dying man's last victory over selfishness bespeaks not merely our pity for him, but our reverence. There is also something profoundly sad in the way in which that desolate heart, after half claiming back the living children, feels that, in real fact, only the dead little one is left it."

No more fitting comment on the poem as a whole has been written than the one by Mr. Luce: "The tragedy is without even the 'dram of eale'; there is no excess or defect of any human passion that might have worked his doom for any. Here no one sins except life itself; and for the evil of bare human life Nemesis may in some sense be reserved."

# 𝔗𝔥𝔢 𝔄𝔠𝔞𝔡𝔢𝔪𝔶 𝔆𝔩𝔞𝔰𝔰𝔦𝔠𝔰.

THE works selected for this series are such as have gained a conspicuous and enduring place in literature. Each volume is edited by a teacher of reputation, whose name is a guarantee of sound and judicious annotation.

**Addison.** *De Coverley Papers.* Edited by Samuel Thurber. Cloth
*Select Essays.* With Macaulay's *Essay on Addison.* Edited by Samuel Thurber. Cloth

**Arnold.** *Essays in Criticism.* Edited by Susan S. Sheridan. Cloth
*Rugby Chapel.* Edited by L. D. Syle. In *Four English Poems.* Cloth

*Sohrab and Rustum.* Edited by George A. Watrous. In *Three Narrative Poems.* Cloth

**Blackmore.** *Lorna Doone.* Edited by R. Adelaide Witham.

**Burke.** *Conciliation with the Colonies.* Edited by C. B. Bradley. Cloth

**Burns.** *Selections.* Edited by Lois G. Hufford. Cloth

**Byron.** *The Prisoner of Chillon.* Edited by L. D. Syle. In *Four English Poems.* Cloth

**Carlyle.** *Essay on Burns.* Edited by H. W. Boynton. Cloth
*Selections.* Edited by H. W. Boynton. Cloth

**Coleridge.** *The Ancient Mariner.* Edited by George A. Watrous. In *Three Narrative Poems.* Cloth

**Cowper.** *John Gilpin's Ride.* Edited by L. D. Syle. In *Four English Poems.* Cloth

**George Eliot.** *Silas Marner.* Edited by W. Patterson Atkinson. Cloth

**Emerson.** *Select Essays and Poems.* Edited by Eva March Tappan. Cloth

**Goldsmith.** *The Vicar of Wakefield.* Edited by R. Adelaide Witham. Cloth
*The Traveller* and *The Deserted Village.* Edited by George A. Watrous. In *Selected Poems.* Cloth

**Gray.** *Elegy Written in a Country Churchyard* and *The Progress of Poesy.* Edited by G. A. Watrous. In *Selected Poems.* Cloth

**Irving.** *Life of Goldsmith.* Edited by R. Adelaide Witham.

**Irving.** *The Sketch-Book*. Edited by E. E. Wentworth. Cloth
   *Selections from The Sketch-Book*. Edited by Elmer E. Wentworth. Cloth

**Lowell.** *Selections. The Vision of Sir Launfal and other Poems*. Edited by Dr. F. R. Lane. Cloth

**Macaulay.** Edited by Samuel Thurber.
   *Essay on Addison; Clive; Johnson; Milton*. Cloth
   *Essay on Chatham*. Boards
   *Essays on Milton and Addison*. One volume, cloth
   *Historical Essays*. Cloth
   *Select Essays*. Cloth

**Milton.** *Minor Poems*. Edited by Samuel Thurber. Cloth
   *Paradise Lost, Books I, II*. Edited by H. W. Boynton. Cloth

**Pope.** *The Rape of the Lock*. Edited by L. D. Syle. In *Four English Poems*. Cloth
   *An Essay on Criticism*. Edited by George A. Watrous. In *Selected Poems*. Cloth

**Scott.** *Ivanhoe*. Edited by A. Marion Merrill. Cloth
   *The Lady of the Lake*. Edited by G. B. Aiton. Cloth
   *Marmion*. Edited by Mary E. Adams. Cloth

**Shakespeare.** Edited by Samuel Thurber. *As You Like It; Macbeth; The Tempest*. Cloth
   *Hamlet* (with Pearson's *Questions on Hamlet*). Cloth
   *Julius Cæsar; Merchant of Venice*. New editions. Cloth

**Stevenson.** *Treasure Island*. Edited by W. D. Lewis. Cloth

**Tennyson.** *Enoch Arden*. Edited by George A. Watrous. In *Three Narrative Poems*. Cloth
   *Idylls of the King*. Edited by H. W. Boynton. Cloth

**Webster.** *Reply to Hayne*. Edited by C. B. Bradley. Cloth

---

**Four English Poems:** *The Rape of the Lock*, *John Gilpin's Ride*, *The Prisoner of Chillon*, and *Rugby Chapel*. Edited by L. D. Syle. Cloth

**Three Narrative Poems:** *The Ancient Mariner*, *Sohrab and Rustum*, and *Enoch Arden*. Edited by G. A. Watrous. Cloth

**Selected Poems** from Pope, Gray, and Goldsmith. Edited by George A. Watrous. Cloth

**The Short Story.** Edited by W. P. Atkinson. Cloth